A VISIBLE HERITAGE

Columbia County, New York

A HISTORY IN ART AND ARCHITECTURE

By Ruth Piwonka and Roderic H. Blackburn

BLACK · DOME

BLACK DOME PRESS CORP.
RR 1, Box 422
Hensonville, New York 12439
Tel: (518) 734-6357
Fax: (518) 734-5802

TWENTIETH ANNIVERSARY EDITION: 1996

Dedicated to Mary Black

This edition of *A Visible Heritage* is made
possible by a grant from Furthermore,
the J.M. Kaplan Fund publication program.

Photograph credits: Pages 27, 43, 47, 50, 60,
65, 68, 74, 88, 90 top, 91, 96, 98 top, 100, 108 left,
123, 128 right, 129, 130 bottom, 137, 142,
152, and 154 by Michael Fredericks, Jr.; pages
140 bottom, 148, 149, and 150 by Fred Van Tassell;
pages 79, 97, 107, 112, 113 top, 114, 115 bottom,
127, and 156 from the Rowles Studio Collection,
Hudson, New York; all other photographs by
Roderic H. Blackburn unless otherwise stated.

Additional credits for this edition: Pages 33,
90 bottom, 94, and 133 bottom by Arthur Baker;
page 69 by Michael Fredericks. The map on page 6
first appeared in *History of Columbia County* by
Captain Franklin Ellis, published in Philadelphia
by Everts and Ensign in 1878.

First published by Black Dome Press Corp. 1996

Library of Congress Cataloging-in-Publication Data

Piwonka, Ruth.
    A visible heritage. Columbia County, New York : a history in
art and architecture / by Ruth Piwonka and Roderic H. Blackburn.
        p.   cm.
    Originally published: Kinderhook, N.Y. : Columbia County
Historical Society, 1977.
    Includes bibliographical references.
    ISBN 1-883789-08-7 (pbk.)
    1. Art, American—New York (State)—Columbia County.
    2. Architecture—New York (State)—Columbia County.
I. Blackburn, Roderic H.
II. Title.
N6530.N72C646 1996
709'.747'39—dc20   96-20746
                                            CIP

Original edition designed by Winston Potter and
produced by the Publishing Center for Cultural Resources,
New York City

Manufactured in the United States of America

A Twentieth Anniversary Edition

by Ruth Piwonka and Roderic H. Blackburn

For all the change brought by the twentieth century, much of Columbia County's visible heritage remains unchanged. Its historic art is preserved in museums and by conscientious collectors and its manmade environment is mostly intact. It is still easy to find quiet old roads that wend around hills toward the Hudson or the Berkshires. Beside them lie traditional farmsteads (many preserved by second home owners), and where the roads intersect some hamlets and villages retain a nineteenth-century aura. Despite innovations that would confound him, Martin Van Buren would recognize most of the village-scape in Kinderhook. Anson Pratt would find the homes of his Frisbee and Eaton neighbors still in place and would delight in recent care for his own in New Concord. Although he might be amazed at the development of Copake, the first lord of Livingston Manor could find his way over now-paved highways to reach the eastern extremities of his domain. Sherman and Lydia Griswold and the Lawrence brothers would feel at ease in their old Spencertown houses, and Simeon Rockefeller would be pleased to enter one of the multiple doorways of his tavern in Germantown. Brother James Meacham would glory in the nineteenth-century development of Mount Lebanon, now mostly unchanged. And Jacob Rutsen Van Rensselaer could look at his Claverack mill and house with a sense of security — if awestruck by the botanical wonderland that now graces his front lawn.

Beginning in the late nineteenth century, events and circumstances well beyond the bounds of Columbia County conspired to create major changes here. The opening of the West, exploitation of the deep soil of the Midwest, and the advent of steam power lured farmers and manufacturing interests away from the Northeast. Mills located on streams throughout the county were abandoned. Today, most have been torn down, and stone walls built to mark newly cleared fields and pastures now run through mature woodlands. If use of the land has changed, the essential character of the landscape is intact, however. In recent years, county residents have fought to preserve this landscape, successfully defeating proposed power plants, a waste incinerator, an oil refinery, a race track, dense developments, and large landfills.

Within the framework of a stable population significant changes in agriculture and manufacture have taken place since the turn of the century. The First World War, a flu epidemic, and the Great Depression have also had their impact. When Columbia County was losing population through the 1930s, an influx of new residents was spurred by the automobile, which brought the county closer to Albany and New York City as suburb and weekend home site. This in-migration has brought with it a higher standard of living and service opportunities for longtime residents. The advances have been tempered, unfortunately by higher taxes.

Other more recent trends reflect the centralization and homogenization of American society. Scattered one-room schoolhouses have given place to centralized schools, reflecting higher education expectations and anticipated efficiency of shared resources. Family farms have continued to disappear, resulting in abandoned fields or more efficient agri-business. The manufacturing base has diminished and diversified, evidence of flagging interest in Columbia County streams as a power source. Main Street mom-and-pop stores have closed as shopping-mall chain stores underprice them. In their place specialty stores supply collectibles, antiques, natural foods, decorator items, and gifts.

The countryside is being left by its farm families and millworkers at the same time that urbanites are leaving the city for the country. The visible effect on the landscape has been the loss of small farms, the expansion of suburban housing, and the dispersal of second-home residences in the appealing hills of the central and eastern townships. Where once dirt roads and two-lane highways served a resident population, four-lane highways now speed up the tempo, bringing weekenders from far afield. Their desire to build has led to local planning and zoning ordinances that set higher or more uniform standards and result in a environment that speaks less of individual initiative than that of the past. New technology, especially information processing, is accelerating these changes by allowing more people to leave the cities but maintain employment tied to them. As the age of machines and farming wanes, services and information are expanding in Columbia County as in the rest of the country.

The growth of professionalized public and private services supports these trends. Where once families and communities relied on themselves in difficult times, now county agencies, hospitals, police, and software technicians answer cries for help. One of the last vestiges of community self reliance is the volunteer fire and rescue squad, still alive and well, cherished for embodiment of the values of an older America as much as for effectiveness.

Twentieth-century Overview

Changes founded on a desire for higher living standards and more efficient use of resources have achieved observable results. They have also had these consequences: a more uniform and homogenized environment, restrictions on use of one's property, higher taxes, and increased cost of construction and services. It is, in short, the catalog of election eve gripes we will predictably share with our neighbors — voicing displeasure at the rising expense that, in turn, gives us the pleasures we stay in Columbia County to enjoy.

Art and Architecture

Houses are structures that have survived the last three hundred years because they have been easily adapted to changes in life. Even electricity (lights and all those labor saving kitchen devices), the telephone, and the motor vehicle have not made old houses obsolete. Indeed, in Columbia County old houses command a premium for their historic style.

Columbia County houses built in the seventeenth and early eighteenth centuries followed tradition closely, emphasizing function over form. More accurately, form followed function; useful features were built attractively by adding small decorative conceits. In the later eighteenth century, with the advent of classical inspiration, decorative appearance became more important. By the nineteenth century, that trend accelerated, with style changes based largely on European prototypes being introduced almost every decade. The mechanization of house building (balloon framing, band saw brackets, etc.) had a lot to do with this frenetic showmanship. Although Federal and Greek Revival styles were national ones, their distinctive form reflected local craftsmanship and aesthetic expression. After the Civil War, Columbia County, like many other places, lost its handmade character. Machine tooled millwork created an architectural uniformity that national styles have never since eluded. However lovely Columbia County Gothic, Queen Anne, and other Victorian styles may be, it is possible to find Michigan, Oregon, and Indiana communities that closely resemble some of what we see here.

The twentieth century saw a significant change in how houses were used and looked. We can thank Thomas Edison for the practical application of electricity at the root of this. Electric lighting in all rooms, indoor plumbing, central heating, and innumerable appliances enabled rooms to expand in function and number. Efficient use of interior space tended to displace a concern for exterior symmetry. Increasingly, the exterior became an afterthought, with wall angles at unexpected places, windows of different sizes in irregular intervals, and facade materials changing without apparent reason.

Not that this century is devoid of style. A rather stylish colonial revival before the First World War was succeeded by a Cape Cod throwback to seventeenth-century New England cottages and a ranch house revival of the Old West inspired by movies of the 1920s, 30s, and 40s. The split ranch that followed the Second World War represented a move toward economy by making the basement a family living room. The formal living room was abandoned to guests — like the *groote kamer* of the eighteenth century and the parlor of the nineteenth. We continue to want one beautiful room that will remain unused except to entertain our superiors.

The economics that moved family living to the basement shaped a persistent trend in construction. In this century houses, on average, have become smaller and simpler in detail. Increasingly, their components are manufactured elsewhere. These are ways to reduce cost while retaining convenient utilities and appliances. Trailers were a logical outgrowth of the trend; mobile in a newly mobile society, completely manufactured, cheap — and with style an afterthought. The trend continues now with manufactured homes displacing on-site construction. Like cars, future homes will be custom ordered — built far away, delivered, and set up on short order in any wanted style, color, and configuration.

The story of Columbia County institutional and commercial structures is quite different. Mostly built in large sizes and for specific purpose in the nineteenth century, they have proven difficult to adapt to modern needs. Urban multi-story schools can become municipal offices (on the theory that adults can climb stairs children should not); multi-story mills are less fortunate. Water power once piled belt driven machinery floor above floor, but electricity and fuel oil allow one-story manufacturing. Mills disappear, but ironically, one Valatie mill has been replaced with a multi-story medical center of remarkably similar configuration; and the early stone and brick mills at Stuyvesant Falls still function for a chemical company founded by Edison. Despite the clarion call of publisher Al Callan and others, the Chatham railroad station remains unused. However, the Hudson armory, without tenants for years, has been revived for the antique trade that has already saved Hudson's Warren Street. The General Worth Hotel, catalyst for preservation of downtown in the 1970s, was lost — but a successful 1990s campaign to save the Hudson Opera House may be the spark that really ignites rejuvenation.

The fate of art in Columbia County is similar to that of architecture. The distinctive regional characteristics of both became increasingly submerged in the national culture of the late nineteenth century. Frederic Church was the premier aesthetic messenger of the Manifest Destiny that simultaneously sought to exploit and preserve natural and human resources. Burt Phillips, who travelled west to record waning Indian cultures, returned at the end of the century to paint the Shakers at Mount Lebanon. Less well known than Church's work, his portrayals of anonymous sitters with emblems of fading cultures serve effectively as the human face of Manifest Destiny.

In this century some local artists continued to record Columbia County scenes and sitters. Cuyler Williams of

Hillsdale painted landscapes with adept liquid style. Sara Freeborn, born and raised in Hudson, became an accomplished marble sculptor. Samantha Huntley spent most of her adult life in Kinderhook painting discerning portraits of local notables — arguably the best characterizations the region has ever seen. Betty Warren founded an art school in Malden Bridge that probably trained more Columbia County artists than all prior schooling. Dunning Powell painted revealing portraits in the style learned from his mentor Eugene Speicher when Powell was a youthful offender at Sing Sing.

But the county is better known for twentieth-century artists who came with other urbanites to find quiet haven here. Occasionally they depicted local subjects, like the old lady and her chicken immortalized by George Luks. Louis Bouche and John Carroll were noted contemporaries in the Old Chatham area, where the latter apparently preferred riding to hounds to handling the brush. Today, minimalist Ellsworth Kelly works here quietly and George Rickey's kinetic sculptures dance on Hand Hollow Road.

After twenty years we are heartened to find there is value and interest in *A Visible Heritage.* When we were preparing the book in 1974-75, the Vietnam War was winding down and the country beginning to prepare for celebrating the majestic Bicentennial of the American Revolution. To look so closely at the county was a joyous and inspiring experience.

We continue to receive material that throws new light on our selections. It is pleasant to report that almost none of this calls for correction. One exception is a November 1812 letter in which William W. Van Ness mentions "moving into my new house" — settling speculation on when Talavera was built.

We are still asked about our selection process — most particularly why we included this building and not that one. We intended to illustrate the broad outlines of Columbia County history in works of art and architecture, and the county is blessed with extant examples. Given a larger book, it would have been easy to add to our selection, but adding would not have addressed any different historical themes.

Using visibility as the criterion for inclusion did result in some regrettable omissions. Products of farms and mills that were consumed or long since discarded would have added to our story. Religion (including religious contention), crime, military affairs, social organizations, and civic institutions all get shorter treatment in our account than their importance warrants. And themes documented in public records, newspapers, travelers' accounts, and correspondence suffer badly — among them land ownership, agriculture, politics, local government, and demography. We failed, for example, to take proper note of the extensive mortgaging of land in 1790s that enabled an unprecedented number of Columbians to own the land they lived on and that ultimately played a role in the Antirent movement and the agricultural expansion of the following century. We missed the proliferation of new towns between 1786 and 1838 that reshaped the political scene. And we neglected demographic evidence of the demise of slavery, the arrival of low-paid British millworkers, and the transfer of social power from descendants of the Dutch to those of Palatines and English. Not all history is visible.

We have wrestled with our choice of a cut-off date. In retrospect, the Civil War might have been the logical one, and we did dwell on some of the war's results: a turned economy, new expression in architecture and art, and a stunning presidential winner-loser. Twenty years ago, 1900 seemed a fine choice, however, when Columbia County seemed to lose its uniqueness and new influences reshaped daily life. It was also the time for which living memory took over — so that spoken recollections could inform our sense of the heritage. We can learn from living witnesses about water-generated electricity being rationed in summer drought and new telephones providing the means to keep chess games alive on long winter evenings. Such post-1900 recollections are now burnished by history, but in 1975 they were more clearly part of the new age.

Second Thoughts

Looking back over the years covered, we can see that many Columbia County individuals and institutions assumed national significance but that disproportionate national growth increasingly dwarfed Columbia County. The relative population figures are dramatic. In 1790, the year of the first U.S. Census, the population of the county was reckoned at 27,732 and that of the entire country at about 4 million. Roughly one of every 140 Americans was in Columbia County. By 1900, when the national population had expanded to almost 76 million, Columbia County residents numbered only 43,211, however; only one out of every 1,760 Americans lived here. The Columbia population has, in fact, been remarkably stable since the end of the eighteenth century — varying between 32,000 and 47,000 throughout the nineteenth century and actually shrinking somewhat before rising to approach 63,000 in the final decade of the twentieth.

It must have been the hundred years of stable population and economic decline that accounts for such a range of fine houses being saved for us. Excepting spurts of remodeling in the 1920s and 1980s, the twentieth century has been kind to our old houses (if not our institutional structures). It is unfashionable and even indiscreet to admire decrease and decline, but the words an anonymous Austrian architect imparted to Oliver Rackham may hold the key to our good fortune: "Neither war nor earthquake is so destructive of historic amenities as too much money." We rejoice in the historic amenities that time has preserved in Columbia County.

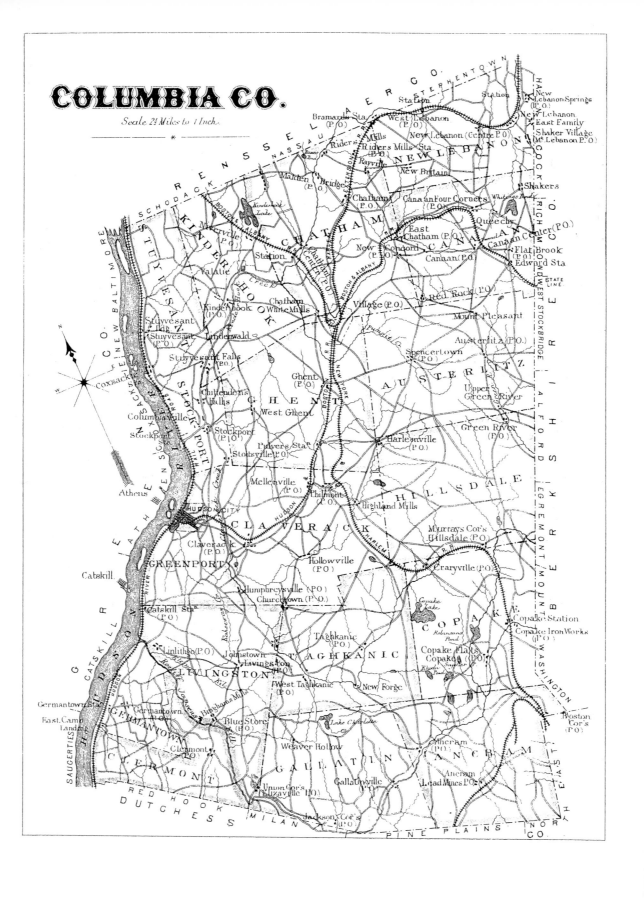

COLUMBIA CO.

Scale 2¼ Miles to 1 Inch.

Contents

CHAPTER 2 CONTINUED OVERLEAF

For Ruth Piwonka and Roderic Blackburn the visible heritage of Columbia County becomes the key to unlock a door that opens on its people, places and events. In this extraordinary collection of the arts and architecture of the region its history is described from the earliest days of settlement to the end of the nineteenth century. Most of the buildings illustrated still stand, readily accessible to contemporary observers as symbols of the people who built them and of the events that their presence conveys. As for the paintings, some are on public view in museums and historical societies but many are reserved in the families for whom they were made. Familiar and hitherto unknown examples alike are presented here in relation to county history. Portraits are illustrated alongside the houses, towns, factories, and public institutions in which the sitters once had so great a stake. Landscapes, genre scenes, and photographs become descriptive adjuncts to the biographies and events that are delineated and celebrated.

The dramatic two-century growth of the region — from land dominated by the original patrician Dutch owners to towns, villages, and one highly successful planned city, in a landscape dotted by mills and crossed by highways and railroads — is all recaptured here. It is unlikely that any reader who passes through Spencertown will fail to remember Mr. Griswold slipping a little salt to the handsomest of his sheep on Sunday evening. Neither will many travel near Hudson without looking for the Federal-style Plumb house that lies hidden beneath the bracketed and Italianate glass of fashion that Dr. Oliver Bronson called home. The Collin residence at Hillsdale will ever invoke the charming tea service with the "picturesque chimney-tops" of the same house in its engravings. In Ghent, Broadstairs will conjure up the tipsy equestrian sheriff who mistook its stairway for the open road. At Lindenwald, Old Kinderhook will be remembered as he improved upon the 1797 house of Peter Van Ness. And who will not search the faces of today's descendants of Dorrs, Van Alstynes, and the five Pruyn children who married five Van Vleck children to find there traces of their ancestors' visages. The mills that still stand, the bridges that still serve, the surviving buildings at the Shakers' Holy Mount — all will be reminders of this wide-ranging compendium of Columbia County history, art, and architecture. It is a delight, a time machine, an instruction.

Mary Black

ADDENDUM

As a loving attendant at the cradle of American art, Mary Black was well acquainted with Columbia County when she wrote the foreword to A Visible Heritage *in 1977. She had already played a major role in recognizing Ammi Phillips as the single artist responsible for four dissimilar groups of early nineteenth-century portraits that included many Columbia County subjects. And she had started the work that would ultimately enable her to name the eighteenth-century limners who recorded the Ten Broecks, Van Alstynes, and Van Alens whose likenesses appear here. After coming to live in Columbia County in 1987, she continued untangling the web of early American portraiture, sorting images and records to reconstruct an all-but-lost New World society. She was planning an exhibition of eighteenth-century portraits that link the Hudson Valley with northern New England, Boston, and Virginia when she died in Germantown, in her home at the Rockefeller Tavern, in February 1992.*

Preface and Acknowledgements

Art and architecture are our visible heritage; they symbolize our history and dramatize the creativity of our past. By emphasizing the relationship between history and the arts, history becomes more interesting and the arts more meaningful. This fact and the conviction that Columbia County has significance beyond its borders provided the inspiration for this book. Here are the ideals, inventions, and creativity which formed our national character and are now benchmarks for the future.

This book reveals the chronological history of Columbia County through 160 examples of the county's art and architecture spanning over two hundred years from the seventeenth through the late nineteenth century. Each object or site is described in terms of its aesthetic qualities and its historic relationship to people and events in Columbia County history.

The suggestion for this book came from a Columbia County Historical Society photographic exhibit in 1974 featuring the visible heritage of Columbia County as an interesting and enjoyable way of introducing school children to their county's history. With the aim of preserving the research from that exhibit in a permanently useful form, we have produced this book. Although other books on the county's history have been published, relatively little has been printed on its architecture or its art. No source, to our knowledge, combines all three elements into an integrated account.

In our selection of objects and sites for inclusion in the book we have been guided by three criteria: (1) importance to Columbia County's political, social, and/or economic development; (2) the quality of the art or architectural style; (3) typical examples of the art and architecture that characterize the mainstream of county life. In each case we have tried to show the significance of each object or site to the people who produced, owned, or used it and the importance of these people to the historic developments of Columbia County. In addition, we have extended the relevance of the book beyond the boundaries of Columbia County by describing its art, and especially its architecture, in terms of its relationship to the development of styles both in the region and in the nation. Introductory sections place the range of Columbia County's visible heritage in the context of American art and architectural history.

Graphic arts predominated our choice of artworks for two reason. First, they advance our general historical purpose by illustrating personalities and scenes of Columbia County; and second, graphic arts have been the principal art in the county from the eighteenth century. The breadth of art in the eighteenth and nineteenth centuries is revealed in family collections that were accumulated by several generations, old published accounts, public records, family histories, and various manuscript materials. Our choice has been limited to approximately seventy-five selections that best reflect (1) major historical trends, (2) art production in the county, (3) uses of art by people of the county, and (4) the variety of art ranging from naive amateur to schooled academic painters. We have tried to restrict examples of landscape paintings to county scenes, and selected examples for their general interest and attractiveness as well as for their capacity to illustrate both the art and general history of Columbia County.

There are over 15,000 buildings in Columbia County from which a choice of less than one hundred has had to be made. The basic criteria for selection has been primarily stylistic and, secondarily, functional. We have tried to choose well-preserved examples that clearly illustrate distinctive features characterizing each style. Most frequently, the larger, more expensively built houses have best illustrated such features. To partially correct this biased picture of Columbia County architecture, we have included some smaller and stylistically simpler buildings that are more representative of the majority of surviving early houses.

As we worked, we began to see some important themes emerging. First, it is quite evident that Columbia County has produced examples of rural art and architecture of unusually high quality compared with those of many neighboring counties. A surprising number of such houses and paintings still survive in the county. Second, we noticed that Columbia County probably has a wider range of architectural and art styles extending over a longer period than almost any other county in upper New York State. This is a reflection not only of the diversity of immigrant groups who settled here but also of the relatively high level of prosperity. The third theme was the discovery of a remarkably pervasive interrelationship of kinship, social, political, and economic ties among the families of Columbia County. This web of life at first characterized individual ethnic groups in the seventeenth and eighteenth centuries. But by the nineteenth century ties between groups, business associations, and political alliances throughout the county, were indispensable to the rapid development of the county in that century.

In conclusion, we see these purposes for the book. It was written for a lay audience — both young and old people with an interest in history, art, and architecture. We hope they find it informative to their understanding of how Columbia County became what it is today. We also hope this book will be useful to school classes, especially those concerned with local and state history. And finally we hope our readers derive as much enjoyment as we have from the daily excitement of finding new works of art and architecture and exploring their relationships to each other.

Georgette Turner has made particular contributions to this book in the area of later nineteenth-century art. Her studies in that period and research into art activity and working artists in Columbia County during that time have enhanced our awareness of the broad social significance of painting during the last seventy years of that century. She has contributed generously her knowledge of painting in the county and prepared most of the material for the appendix.

Mary Black, Curator of Paintings, Sculpture, and Decorative Arts at The New-York Historical Society has graciously prepared the foreword. Her studies of Pieter Vanderlyn, Ammi Phillips, and Erastus Salisbury Field have been informative and inspiring works. Her interest and knowledge of Columbia County are of long standing.

Michael Fredericks, Jr., is responsible for many of the fine photographs and most of the photographic prints. The quality of his work is clearly apparent throughout the book.

The Board of Directors of the Columbia County Historical Society has been most supportive throughout the preparation of the book. Local historians have also helped. Two, who are now deceased, have left copious notes, articles and valuable collections of manuscript material. One of these was Mrs. Frank Rundell of Spencertown; the other, Miss Louise Hardenbrook of Valatie, for many years librarian at the Columbia County Historical Society.

Many conversations with Mrs. Katherine Burgess have aided our identification of individuals and their property in the Kings District. Mr. Walter Miller, Columbia County Historian, has provided information and useful commentary on several specific questions.

Mrs. Allen J. Thomas has had extraordinary patience with our forays through the Columbia County Historical Society Library, an outstanding reference library for New York and local historical and genealogical materials. Other local resources for historical research are the Columbia County Courthouse; the New York State Library, Albany; the library of the Albany Institute of History and Art; and the Albany County Courthouse. The staffs at these places have been most helpful.

Researchers and historians whose efforts are listed in the bibliography have laid important groundwork for parts of this book.

Museum and related society staffs outside the county have helped in providing information or photographs of art objects. Those who have been especially helpful are: Richard S. Allen, Office of State History, New York State Department of Education; The American Museum in Britain; Lynn Beebe, New York State Division for Historic Preservation; William Campbell, The National Gallery; Jane B. Davies, Avery Library; Dr. William Emerson, Franklin D. Roosevelt Library; Margot Gayle, Friends of Cast-Iron Architecture; Cheryl Gold, Clermont State Historic Site; Hendrik Hudson Chapter of the DAR; Dr. Leo Hershkowitz, Historical Documents Collections, Queens College; Barbara Luck and Cynthia Seibels, Abby Aldrich Rockefeller Folk Art Collection; Richard Cox, Maryland Historical Society; Linda McClean, Olana State Historic Site; Robert Meader, The Shaker Museum; Norman S. Rice, Albany Institute of History and Art; City Art Museum of Saint Louis; Mildred E. Steinbach, Frick Art Reference Library; Paul Stambach, Fort Crailo State Historic Site; William Verner, The Adirondack Museum; James L. Whitehead, formerly at the Franklin D. Roosevelt Library.

Many individuals have graciously permitted us to photograph their homes, buildings, and paintings. Often they have made available the information they have about the object and its past history. We are particularly indebted to the following: William and Jean Appell, Richard Barker, Hendryk Booraem, Albert Callan, Gretchen Coons, Harrison Cultra, Edward and Friedl Ekert, A. Donald Emerich, Mildred Finch, Walter Finch, Edward and Priscilla Frisbee, Rodney Gage, Adelaide and Phyllis Galician, Terry Hallack, Alice P. Kenney, R. G. Kreitzer, Henry and Maria Livingston, Sybil May, Hugh McLelland, William F. McDonald, Lt. Col. Donald E. Mitchell, Florence Niles, Joseph and Nellie Ptaszek, Van Ness and Julia Philip, Ross and Mildred Pigott, C. Woodrow Pulver, Joseph G. Rayback, Margaret Richardson, Charles and Helen M. Rundell, John Schott, Margaret Schram, Stein Soelberg, Cornelia Ten Broeck, Allen J. and Mary Thomas, John Weinman, Charlotte Wilcoxen. For copy editing we are grateful to Gail Battles.

We are, in addition, especially grateful to the New York State Council on the Arts for their initial grant covering the cost of preparing the manuscript for printing and to M. J. Gladstone and Francis F. Dobo of the Publishing Center for Cultural Resources for diligence and judgment in seeing that the manuscript became the publication that it is today.

Ruth Piwonka
Roderic H. Blackburn

Kinderhook, N.Y.
1976

ADDENDUM

We must add to the above Sharon Palmer, Executive Director of the Columbia County Historical Society, for so effectively handling administrative details pertaining to this edition, and Helen McLallen, Curator, for so much assistance in relocating and arranging for the reprinting of a number of photographs. We are also grateful to Mike Gladstone for doing it all over again. And we are especially grateful to Furthermore, the J. M. Kaplan Fund publication program, and its Director, Joan K. Davidson, for the personal interest and encouragement she has given this project.

R.P. and R.H.B., 1996

The character of Columbia County lands has greatly affected the development of life in the county. The adjacent Hudson River, from the time of discovery through the late nineteenth century has been a source of transportation and occupations. People of diverse backgrounds and ambitions have lived and worked in the county. The land, the river, and the people form a varied history.

Columbia County is located on the eastern bank of the Hudson River about 110 miles above its mouth. The western section of the county is comprised of rolling land that is part of the fertile Hudson valley. Hilly terrain begins in the central part of the county, and the ground rises to the Taconic range at the eastern edge. Fast-moving streams are found in all localities.

First to inhabit these lands were the Mahican Indians. Before the Europeans came, this tribe had been engaged in war with the Iroquois; and by the time settlers began to buy land in the region, the Indian population had already dwindled greatly.

In 1609, when Henry Hudson explored the river, notice was given to the region; but the first recorded purchases of land from the Indians did not occur until forty years later when Kiliaen Van Rensselaer purchased a large tract of land called Claverack comprising more than a third of the central part of the county. Claverack lands, at the river's edge, however, were actually owned by others; and the patroon's claim and rights were strongly contested. Inland, however, Van Rensselaer leased farm-sized lots to settlers. Lands at Kinderhook in the upper third of the county were purchased by individuals and small groups of freeholders during the 1660s. After 1664, when the English captured New Netherlands, Dutch landowners had to reestablish their land titles by obtaining patents from the English governor. Finally, during the 1680s, Robert Livingston, a Scotsman educated in the Netherlands, purchased large tracts of lands in the southern third of the county. In 1715, his lands were given manor status: besides

the right to lease lands, he had direct authority to govern his domain under this English system. In the year 1686, the thirty-one patentees at Kinderhook were granted self-government in the form a town system, also derived from English practice.

All the tracts of land patented in this period extended approximately twenty miles "easterly into the woods." Since the population was small, dependent on the river for transportation, and principally interested in agriculture and timbering, only land in the western part of the county was developed. Good water power existed at falls, and grain and timber could be conveniently processed at the mills established there. In the 1730s, the expanding population of New England needed more land. New Englanders who settled the Berkshire and Taconic mountains caused much friction because of prior Dutch claims. In 1772 the King arbitrarily settled the argument in favor of the New Englanders.

Considering the amount of dissension over ownership of land in the eastern part of the county, the remarkable cooperation between Dutch and New Englanders from early 1775 through the period until the Battle of Saratoga is surprising. On one side, the Tories organized so effectively that Continental troops were called to suppress insurrection. On the other side were determined patriots who persisted in undermining Tory operations. Besides this, farmers and merchants in the region met the seemingly endless requirements of food, supplies, and transportation for the militia and Continental soldiers who awaited the English attack that finally came at Saratoga in the fall of 1777. After the battle, many tensions were relaxed; and thereafter most Tories were swiftly dealt with. Besides involvement in local conspiracies and the war efforts, some individual members of the Livingston family participated directly in the proceedings of the Continental Congress; and Matthew Adgate of the Kings District was an influential delegate to New York's Provincial Congress.

Columbia
County
History

13

After the Revolution, the county began its most dramatic period of development. In 1784 a band of Quaker merchant-seamen arrived from the New England coast and purchased land from the Dutch at Claverack Landing. Their plan for an entirely new city with an economy based on shipping, seal-fishing, and allied ship-building industries was an overnight success. The city of Hudson quickly became the center of commercial and social life in Columbia County. In 1809 the enterprising Quakers formed the Columbia Manufacturing Society and hired an English mechanic to direct cotton mills at Columbiaville, putting the county in the forefront of the Industrial Revolution in America.

In contrast to the profit-oriented commerce and lively, elegant atmosphere of the port city, another band of settlers established a community organized around large communal families and strict religious prescriptions. The Shakers, led by Mother Ann Lee who first came to America in 1774, had gained many converts in the northeastern part of the county at New Lebanon in 1779–80. After her death at Watervliet in 1784, her converts went on to establish austere, industrious communities whose reputation soon spread throughout America and Europe.

Columbia County was formally created out of parts of Albany County in 1786. At Claverack, the first county seat, a new courthouse was built. There and elsewhere in the county, experiments tested the new laws of the young nation. The first generation of Columbia County lawyers reflected the somewhat aristocratic attitudes of the Federalist government leaders. But men of Martin Van Buren's generation came from a different background and by the 1820s were able to effect further modifications in the system of government at county and state levels. By the 1830s and 1840s such changes were found at the national level, too, when Jackson, and then Van Buren, became president. During the 1840s, the Anti-Rent Movement successfully challenged civic and legal authority in the county and state. In Columbia County the Livingston Manor was finally broken up after more than 150 years. By the middle of the century some dreams of common people were beginning to come true. To protect them, Samuel Tilden, a brilliant political economist and New York governor from Lebanon Springs, instituted reforms attacking the corruption that had infiltrated the patronage system introduced by Van Buren.

The effects of the Industrial Revolution in Columbia County, as elsewhere, were mixed. Robert Fulton's steamboat, *North River* (later called *Clermont* for his benefactor's estate) heralded its beginnings in Columbia County. Columbiaville set a precedent for industry in the county. The railroads

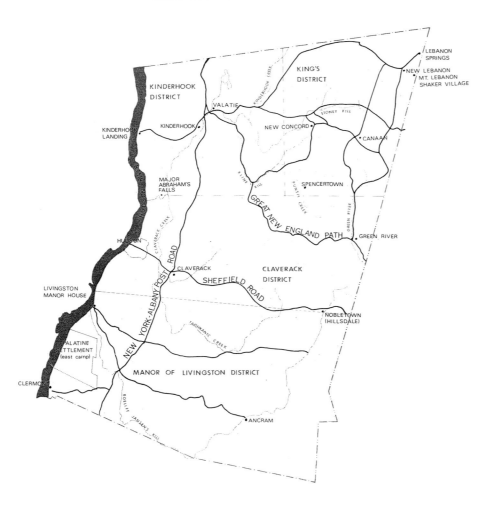

Columbia County in 1786, the year it was formed from Albany County. The districts shown, which were established in 1772, were superseded by eight townships in 1788. District boundaries, main roads, principal creeks, and eighteenth-century settlements are shown in their approximate locations.

14

began to crisscross the county in 1837 and opened heretofore isolated areas to improved transportation for farm and manufactured products. With more reliance on mechanics and less on natural resources, the Industrial Revolution could happen almost anywhere — especially where labor was cheap. By the end of the nineteenth century large-scale manufacturing had begun to move away from the county, and once again the county's major enterprise was agriculture.

Columbia County's history has been varied. The different backgrounds and abilities of the people who have lived here have contributed to success in a wide range of endeavors; and the mingling of Dutch, English, and New England traditions did, in the long run, turn out quite well. The growth and development of the entire nation have, of course, affected life in the county. The agriculture and mills, having lasted from the colonial period until the present day, create a continuity with the past.

Columbia County has a remarkably rich and varied art history that is representative of many facets of American art from the beginning to the present day. Paintings of the eighteenth and nineteenth centuries exhibit a great variety of style largely attributable to the European, and especially the English, heritage that settlers brought with them and that later immigrants renewed. Even after the Revolution, art in America did not experience immediate independence, although it did begin assuming distinctive characteristics.

Two major traditions make up the European background that was brought to colonial America. The first of these is the medieval tradition, generally associated in its origin with England and the northern European countries. It arose in societies governed by superstition, practical experience, and intense religious experience. The art of this tradition is characterized by the representation of things as they are, by varied use of proportion, and by brightness and color. Religious sentiment dominated the medieval idea of beauty: painting simply represented the beauty that was in all creation. Aesthetic values were not developed and the idea that a thing itself was beautiful did not exist.

The other tradition that affected European culture was the classical, which derived from the Greek and Roman civilizations. The classical tradition grew out of societies that had time for leisure and were enquiring and speculative in their attitude toward life. Because of its apparent intellectual progress, this tradition, historically, has been more admired and used in many different ways from the Middle Ages through the twentieth century. Each succeeding period has interpreted the forms of ancient Greece and Rome in its own way, each age believing its own to have the best comprehension of Graeco-Roman culture. The Italian Renaissance, that great classical revival, moved slowly over Europe; but it was not until the late seventeenth century that its full force was established in England and other northern European countries. By the eighteenth century the English and French believed not only in artistic beauty but also in beauty as a pure abstraction that could be objectively defined and governed by rules. In painting and sculpture the various subjects an artist could render were ranked in importance, and each was assigned a prescribed format.

The settlers who first came to the upper Hudson valley, and those who followed for the next hundred years, were Dutch and English; and all were direct descendants of the historic medieval tradition. From the beginnings of art in the region that is now Columbia County, classical influences came from England, where classical models were newly fashionable. The first sustained period of American art occurred in the Hudson valley during the first half of the eighteenth century. Portraits from this period are the most notable survivors today, although inventories and wills from that time indicate that a variety of subjects decorated colonial homes. While no native seventeenth-century paintings are documented from the upper Hudson valley, both paintings and prints were imported for use here at least as early as the 1670s. The seventeenth-century Dutch settlers' love for paintings was a value kept alive by their eighteenth-century descendants and was probably a factor in the burst of native painting that occurred in the first decades of the eighteenth century. The patroon portraits (so-called because they portray likenesses of leading Hudson valley families) initially imitated the composition, posture, and gen-

Art in Columbia County

15

eral format of the English mezzotint portraits. Such printed portraits reflected a classically inspired idealistic beauty, and the composition and posture of the subjects differed greatly from the stylized portraiture of the medieval tradition. In the second quarter of the century, however, some portraits returned to the conventionalized medieval format: stiff, erect posture; decorated surfaces; and symbolic iconography.

After 1750, with the arrival in New York of several English painters trained in the current classical fashion, the character of portraiture in the Hudson valley was altered. Though not the most accomplished painters England had produced, these men demonstrated an ability to render shapes and textures more realistically and thereby introduced new classically inspired standards to American art. A few Americans from other colonies went to England to learn these new techniques.

A unique record of American attitudes toward art is found in the writings of Peter Van Schaack (1747–1832), whose background was a distinctive mix of Hudson valley cultures. From his predominantly Dutch rural village of Kinderhook he was the first youth to receive college training (Kings College, where the curriculum included aesthetic instruction). Besides the Dutch language, which was used locally throughout the eighteenth century, he wrote a clear, well-reasoned English prose and was a Latin scholar his entire life. His memoranda and diaries from the period of his seven-year exile at the time of the American Revolution are published in *The Life of Peter Van Schaack, LL.D.;* and they reveal that, in spite of the prevailing classical fashion, he embraced the whole of English culture and recognized that it would affect Americans for a long time. His response to English painting in particular gives some insight into American attitudes toward art. The greatest personal enthusiasm he expressed was for the windows in Westminster Abbey:

The colors are vastly beautiful, and of an endless variety, no two of them being exactly alike; the light which is admitted through them is extremely pleasing to the sight, and the most interesting scenes from sacred history are there painted.

For Van Schaack, art produced by the medieval tradition still worked.

In the contemporary English painting of the day, he admired its technical virtuosity and found the paintings executed with an excellence "carried to a degree of perfection of which [he] had no idea that they were capable." He appreciated the classicists' capability to imitate nature so perfectly; but expressing the rather puritanical view that realism ought not be carried so far, he rejected nudity in art inspired by Greek and Roman models. He also expressed disgust at the "strange mixture of sacred and profane, serious and ridiculous" in rooms where paintings were exhibited. He felt that in England, "The arts of luxury and the refinements of pleasure are, indeed, carried to an excess from which we (thank God) are as yet far distant."

What Peter Van Schaack admired and what he disclaimed tend to reveal the American viewpoint in art during the Federal Period (1783–1830). Subsequent art history shows that Americans continued to observe more restrained rules of decorum in their portraits and other paintings. In the eighteenth century *decorum* was a special term denoting the appropriate and seemly representation of a subject. American decorum, established in the early years of the new nation, apparently carried a stronger element of propriety with a moral connotation. When artists like Gilbert Stuart and John Trumbull returned from their European sojourns, their enthusiastic patrons eagerly sought only finely painted appropriate subjects, usually portraits. The idealistically inspired classical nude was simply not acceptable. Even provincial portraitists, like A. Phillips and E. S. Field, of the later Federal Period and after were restrained by the decorum and format established by Copley and Stuart.

Independence in America at this time was fostered by national pride, by the effects of increasing education, and by improving economic conditions. National pride inspired a rash of historical paintings and numerous portraits of leading citizens. These followed the prescribed classical format. Such paintings represented the high style of American art and were not equaled for a long time. The excellence of technique, which so astonished Peter Van Schaack, became a standard sought after by those who could afford it.

In addition, education was becoming widespread by 1800. Following English models, academy training included art instruction, which strengthened the awareness of and desire for art in American life. At this same time the nation was also expanding economically. While many could not afford the fine works of Stuart, Copley, and Vanderlyn, they could readily afford the art produced by a growing number of painters whose work ranged between art and decorative painting. Some of these painters were native Americans who had had the opportunity to study the work of their European-trained colleagues. Still others were Europeans who, in this period, came to visit and sometimes stayed to paint the people and the land of the United States.

Conscious efforts to promote art were made by Chancellor Robert R. Livingston and his brother, Edward Livingston, at that time mayor of New York City. In 1803 Robert R. Livingston became the first president of the American Academy, which eventually was overshadowed by the National Academy. One of the Academy's first endeavors was to arrange for the purchase of European paintings and plaster casts of antique classical sculpture, which were exhibited publicly in America.

The art of the American Federal Period is most lively and diverse. In spite of the classical restraints and the moral prohibitions against certain subjects, native energy and talent created lively and colorful renderings of people and places. This art did not end abruptly at the close of the Federal Period. Instead it expanded in quantity as the nation grew and spread westward. Ideals and goals set by formal organizations like the American Academy were adopted by the general population.

In the 1830s, a period when American politics and society moved toward more democratic practice, American art renewed its independence. In portraiture many more Americans demonstrated a preference for greater realism. By this time there were a greater number of skilled painters who worked in this style. Many art students had an opportunity to travel to Europe. They questioned the classical rules and, like Peter Van Schaack, looked at the whole of European art. Painters in Europe and America grew in self-esteem and became professional artists in theory as well as in practice. One exception was Hudson-born Francis Edmonds, who was a banker and art patron and a fine genre painter in his own right. He enjoyed the status of accomplished amateur ("lover") in the true sense of the word. Another Columbia County native, Luman Reed, made a distinctive contribution to American art in the period; as a successful New York City merchant, he began to purchase contemporary works of art and exhibit them in his own public gallery. By patronizing the artist and by providing public exposure, Reed contributed greatly to the success of painters like Thomas Cole, the first influential artist of the Hudson River school.

Although he did not work in Columbia County, Thomas Cole was influential in the development of landscape painting and in the subsequent course of art in America, Columbia County included. Recalling works of old Italian masters, Cole wrote,

. . . they were gifted with a keen perception of the beautiful in nature, and imitated it in simplicity. They did not sit down, as the modern artist often does, with a preconceived notion of what is or ought to be beautiful. . . . I do not believe that they theorized, as we do; they loved the beauty that they saw around them. (Dunlap, II, 365)

Not only did Cole oppose the eighteenth-century view that beauty could be objectively defined, but he also challenged the supremacy of portraiture and history painting, for he saw them as examples of human vanity. Instead he believed that the natural beauty of the landscape was important and that "to circumscribe it with a gilt frame" required particularly truthful representation.

Although portraiture and history painting continued, they did decline as major genres with the advent of the camera in 1840. Freed from their responsibility to record faces and events, painters began to experiment with light, color, and atmospheric effects in landscapes. These painters were trained in formal aspects of design and, as Cole noted, began with some preconceived ideas of beauty and organized their compositions with a balance of elements and color.

By the 1850s, landscape painting was sought after and the desire for portraits and painted decorations began to decline. Resident artists like Henry Ary and Arthur Parton of Hudson produced works for county residents, taught painting, and also exhibited work in New York. Landscape painting was not restricted to Hudson River scenes. In the summertime, artists equipped with newly invented portable paints took to the road traveling to other areas of the county, the country, and the world. As a result, new artists came to the county to paint and county-born artists worked outside the county. Landscape painting dominated the latter part of the nineteenth-century county art, although more experimental approaches to it were emphasized. Representation of the subtle effects of light on color became an important aspect.

American landscape painting was the first major break from dependency on European culture. The views of Cole and other American painters were in accord with nineteenth-century romantic philosophies in Europe; thus American painting gained an intellectual status that had heretofore been lacking in earlier native art. In this period, Columbia County's own landscapes along the Hudson and in the eastern mountainous parts attracted painters who traveled from urban centers into rural and scenic regions. From the time that Frederic E. Church arrived and settled permanently outside of Hudson, artists and sculptors have ever since come to reside in the county.

Columbia County Architecture
Columbia County has an unusually rich architectural heritage. Representative and exceptional buildings of all types have been built since the seventeenth century, and a surprising number of early ones survive. In fact, Columbia County probably has the widest range of early architecture still to be found in the upper Hudson River valley, for the county has been prosperous enough to maintain its heritage but not so properous as to pave over its its past with overdevelopment.

There are a number of ways to look at architecture: through its functional use, through its structural form, from its stylistic appearance, and from its historical antecedants. Since the purpose of this book is to record the history of the surviving aesthetic objects in our man-made environment, our discussion is largely concerned with the history of style. The word *style* in this context refers to the arrangement of lines and mass that gives a building a distinctive appearance both inside and out. Buildings constructed with similar principles of design and proportion are said to be of the same style.

This section reviews the history of architectural styles: how each style developed in Europe, how each was adopted in America, and what distinctive or representative examples of each style survive in Columbia County today. Until the twentieth century, there were basically only two sources for the architecture of Columbia County, indeed for all architecture in America and in Europe. These sources were the medieval Gothic tradition from northern Europe and the classical Roman and Greek traditions from the Mediterranean area. All styles of buildings in the seventeenth, eighteenth, and nineteenth centuries came from these two sources. Before the 1750s, all the houses in Columbia County were New World adaptations of houses built for centuries in England and Holland in the medieval Gothic manner. They shared many characteristics with houses built in the Gothic Revival period of the 1840s and 1850s. All the other buildings in Columbia County up until the twentieth century received their inspiration directly or indirectly from classical traditions ultimately derived from the great public buildings of Rome and Greece. These include the styles we call Georgian, Federal, Greek Revival, Italianate, Second Empire, and several others. Within these two traditions of buildings, each change in style was a matter of reworking old ideas with new variations. Sometimes the variations are so different that their common elements are not immediately apparent, but they are there for the interested student to rediscover.

In addition to style, the use or function of buildings is an important part of the study of their architecture. Surviving in Columbia County is a wide range of buildings built for different functions. In addition to domestic structures (homes, privies, gazebos, well houses), there are agricultural buildings (barns, chicken coops, corn cribs), commercial buildings (stores, shops), industrial buildings (mills, manufacturing plants, warehouses), public buildings (courts, jails, schools, firehouses), and what might be called association buildings (churches, taverns, resorts, fraternal and communal structures). Most of these functional types were built in the prevailing architectural style of their periods. We have tried to illustrate at least one example of the more plentiful types, like houses and churches, in the various styles in which they were built. In addition, to complete the full range of environmental arts, we include illustrations of such things as bridges, dams, gravestones, and weathervanes that bridge the gap between art and architecture.

The Medieval Tradition

The first settlers in what is now Columbia County arrived about 1650 from nearby Albany seeking lands to purchase for farming and for speculation outside the boundaries of the Van Rensselaer Manor (within which they could only lease land). On the land overlooking the fertile creek plains these first Dutch settlers built one- and two-room houses, simple houses that were local adaptations of houses built in Holland for centuries before. Indeed some of the oldest houses surviving in Holland have some features in common with houses built in Columbia County as late as 1750, an extraordinary persistence of culture. These American Dutch houses, like their medieval prototypes in northern Europe (as well as in Holland), have a simple floor plan of one or two usually square rooms with an open or free-hung fireplace in the gable end of each room. These unusual fireplaces are unique to American houses built by the Dutch. They consist of a wide funnel-like chimney starting at the ceiling level. There are no sides or jambs to the fireplace (see p. 34) as is the case with English and New England fireplaces of the seventeenth and eighteenth centuries. The structural framing of both Dutch and English medieval type houses is massive — heavy exposed wall posts supporting exposed ceiling joists or beams and a steeply pitched gable roof. Dutch houses have separate entry doors for each room while English style houses (p. 53) have one front door in the center of the house opening onto a vestibule with rooms to either side and a stairway in the middle. Behind the stairway in the center of the English house was a massive central chimney for fireplaces facing into each room. Dutch houses were quite different in this respect; there was usually a separate chimney for each fireplace, and these were most often located at opposite ends of the house. New England or English style houses tended to be a full two stories and were made of wood. Dutch houses were more often just one and a half stories high and were made of stone, brick or wood. With both types, and indeed for all medieval Gothic dwellings, the decorative effect of the house, both exterior and interior, was predominantly a result of the exposure of its structure to full view. Posts, beams, and door and window frames, often brightly painted and sometimes with a molded surface, give these houses their distinctive decorative quality. In contrast, later Georgian houses relied on nonstructural features like panel walls, carving, wallpaper, and a wide range of colors to create their own decorative style. This contrast points out a distinctive feature of medieval homes: their ornamentation is above all a functional expression of their basic structure; what is decorative usually has a functional purpose (like iron wall anchors), and what is functional is usually expressed in a pleasing manner.

Georgian Elegance

The Georgian style of architecture in America derived from a style popular in England during the seventeenth and eighteenth centuries. It became a model for American social and cultural life during the eighteenth century. By then, for the first time, all the colonies began to take on a common visual identity that had been missing during the previous century of regional medieval styles of building.

Georgian domestic architecture is derived from the buildings of the Renaissance, which were themselves adaptations of classical Roman public buildings with emphasis on symmetry, formality, and typical Roman motifs. Even at that the Renaissance took its Roman models indirectly from the writings of Vitruvious, a Roman whose ten-volume work *De architectura* was the only writing on architecture to survive antiquity. Rediscovered in the sixteenth century by an Italian, Andrea Palladio, it became his "sole master and guide" for a new form of architecture based on classical forms. Palladio's Renaissance villas, through his widely read publications, greatly influenced architectural design in Europe, and especially in England. There Palladio's disciples Inigo Jones, Christopher Wren, and others wrote and illustrated books on "Palladian" architecture and created a building mania for a new style of country homes and townhouses in the noble class after the restoration of Charles II in 1660. When the classical Georgian architecture (named for the English monarchs of the eighteenth

19

century) was transplanted to American in the late seventeenth century and became fashionable in what is now Columbia County between the 1760s and 1790s, its form had been altered by its adaptation to the American culture and environment.

As with all styles of architecture following the medieval period, Georgian designs came to America in the illustrated books of English architects published in the first half of the eighteenth century. With these drawings of elevations, floor plans and details, gifted American housewrights and their patrons adapted English Palladian designs to their own needs, means, and environment. Although no pure Italian Palladian houses were ever built in America, concepts of that design are to be seen in most houses built in Columbia County in the era just before and after the Revolution. The Palladian window, pedimented door, hipped roof, and square four-room plan are all a part of this heritage. The Van Schaak (p. 53) and Van Rensselaer (p. 58) mansions are the most fully developed examples of a late Georgian adaptation of Palladian designs. Other houses, like the Johannes Van Alen house (p. 38), represent a more provincial Georgian style in this area, a style owing its more modest scale (only one room deep) and structure (one and a half stories high) to the Dutch heritage of New York. The double slanted, or gambrel, roof of this type of house, however, is not Dutch. In America this type of roof first became popular in the late seventeenth century in New England and was shortly thereafter copied by the Dutch near New York City. The upper Hudson River valley did not adopt the cultural designs of New York City until as much as a half century later.

Examples of Georgian style also persisted in Columbia County well past the Revolution, one example being the Gilbert house of 1794 (p. 92). Indeed the Palladian window was incorporated into many Federal houses, some built as late as 1820. This conservatism of adopting styles long after they had become accepted in urban centers (and continuing to use them when long out of fashion elsewhere) is especially characteristic of the upper Hudson.

The Federal Republic

After defeating the British in battle and discarding the ideas of monarchy, aristocracy, and an established church, the United States was ready for a new cultural image to go with its new political status. It was only natural that the new nation should turn for inspiration to the earliest democracies — Greece and the Roman Republic. A new country needed a new architecture to house its government and express its republican ideals. The classical orders of these early civilizations were aptly suited to these needs; and, as a result, a new classical revival began to sweep America, a revival derived not from Palladian interpretations but rather from the ancient buildings themselves. Thomas Jefferson became a leading exponent of the new Federal style. While Minister to France in the 1780s, he had marveled at the beauty of Roman structures and resolved to shape America's architecture in this direction because, as he put it, ". . . its object is to improve the taste of my countrymen, to increase their reputation, to reconcile them to the respect of the world, and procure them its praise." His desires were amply gratified by an expanding and expansive nation, which populated its cities with countless public buildings in the new style.

Cultural traditions, on the other hand, die hard, even in a revolution. Although Jefferson had envisioned a new architecture drawn directly from ancient Rome, most Americans were not about to give up — revolution or not — their habit of borrowing architectural styles from Britain. Much of our "Federal" style is, in fact, based on adaptations from classical designs popularized by Robert and James Adam in England in the 1760s and 1770s. These talented men, like Jefferson, were inspired with what had been rediscovered about Roman architecture at the excavations of Pompeii and Herculaneum in the mid-eighteenth century. In 1773 they published *The Works of Architecture* in which they copied and adapted Roman designs for contemporary buildings. Compared to the then-current Palladian classicism, the Adam brothers' classical revival was much closer to the original. For the standard Palladian motifs, they substituted "a beautiful variety of light mouldings, gracefully formed, delicately enriched, and arranged with propriety and skill." From the Roman originals they borrowed a decorative scheme emphasizing a variety of pale colors relieved with white ornaments of spidery low-relief trails and scrolls, oval and round medallions, and bas-reliefs of classical figures. By the 1790s the combined influence of Adam designs and original Roman architecture gave birth to America's first national architecture — the Federal style. As in England, the new style was visually more delicate and refined than Georgian designs; functionally it was more flexible and specialized. The traditional square room gave place to elliptical, octagonal, and rectangular shapes. New types of specialized rooms were incorporated into the plan: pantries, closets, and indoor privies.

A few talented architects in America were largely responsible for the development of Federal architecture. Thomas Jefferson has already been mentioned. His home, Monticello, and the University of Virginia, both of which he designed, are landmarks of this neoclassical style. Charles Bulfinch (1763–1844), America's first professional architect, had been introduced to classical architecture in France by Jefferson and then was influenced by the decorative and spacial possibilities of Adam designs when he reached London. Returning to Boston, Bulfinch became the leading architect in that city. The Massachusetts State House (1795–1800), the inspiration for so many later capitol buildings across the country, was his design. In 1796 one of his disciples, Asher Benjamin, published *The Country Builder's Assistant,* the first original book on architecture in this country. In its many editions, this book had a profound influence on architecture, especially domestic architecture in New England. Here were all the designs and instructions the rural housewrights in towns and villages needed to build their patrons' homes.

North of Boston, Samuel McIntire of Salem was, like Bulfinch, designing and building important houses in the new style for wealthy merchants and shippers. At this same time a group of New England shipping merchants left the New England coast for the inland haven of the Hudson River and founded, in 1784, the city of Hudson in Columbia County. They brought with them the new architecture of the coast as evidenced by the Hathaway house (p. 79), which so clearly relates to Samuel McIntire's Salem houses. By doing so they introduced to this county what would become its most popular architectural style.

The Federal style is well represented in Columbia County by houses built between the 1790s and the 1820s. These houses are of brick or clapboard, two stories high with a pitched roof. Rarely do they have more than one room on either side of a center hall. Many are rather simple houses with only the slightest ornamentation, while others, like the Hogeboom (p. 81), Pratt (p. 94) and Vanderpoel (p. 69) houses, are replete with decorations that follow closely the classical motifs popularized by the Adam brothers. In addition, there are a number of rather unusual, perhaps unique, Federal houses in Columbia County. These seem to have some characteristics in common with the works of Benjamin Latrobe, a leading architect south of New York. For example, the central mass of the Joab Center house (p. 83) is oval; the William Van Ness house (p. 66) emphasizes flanking wings; and the Jacob R. Van Rensselaer house (p. 67) is built around two octagonal front rooms. In all three houses the traditional center hall has been dispensed with to create unusual and functionally innovative arrangements.

Beginning about 1810, large factories and mills built along the main streams brought Columbia County into the Industrial Revolution. The largest and most ambitious may have been the mills of the Columbia Manufacturing Society at Columbiaville (p. 100), where buildings of several stories, workshops, and workers' houses were all done in the Federal style. This style, more than any other, proved to be adaptive to different functions, sizes, and decorative treatments. Its versatility accounts, in part, for its wide popularity and for the survival of more houses of this style than any other in Columbia County.

The Greek Revival
The advent of the Greek Revival style seems to have followed the same pattern as the Georgian and Federal styles: ancient ruins were rediscovered and written about and then became the inspiration for architectural adaptations, first in England and later in America. In the case of the Greek style, in 1762, two Englishmen, Stuart and Revetts, published a book called *Antiquities of Athens,* in which they illustrated existing ancient Greek buildings. From this, an interest in Greek architecture first developed in England, but it was in the United States that it came to dominate architecture as no

21

other style before or since. It began in this country with Benjamin Latrobe's design for the Bank of Philadelphia in 1798, the first structure in the New World to be built upon Greek inspiration. The bank was followed in 1811–19), again in Philadelphia, by a major engineering and architectural achievement: Latrobe's Philadelphia Waterworks. The buildings that housed the pumps were done in impeccable classical Greek style. Philadelphia's association with this style is also distinguished by the fact that the largest Greek Revival structure in the world was built there: the Philadelphia Museum of Art (1925).

However, it was not until the 1820s, after the Federal style had run its course, that the Greek style became the dominant architectural mode in this country. Its popularity grew by its association with America's sympathy for the Greek War of Independence against Turkish domination in the 1820s. In addition, America was undergoing a civic revolution of its own in extending suffrage to almost all white adult males instead of only to the privileged and wealthy. It was an era of participatory democracy, the Age of Jackson in which the new style of architecture aptly reflected the virtues of our civic model — Ancient Greece.

It was also the era of population expansion and western migration. The Greek Revival style became the architecture that distinguished our western expansion. It became widespread for another, more practical, reason as well: it was highly adaptive for private as well as public structures, and a simple country house (p. 116) looked just as appropriate in this style as a large courthouse (p. 107). Although many Greek Revival structures were built in the temple style of a pedimented portico of several columns, many other buildings embodied the Greek style in the sense that they adopted some Greek motifs such as small porticos (p. 110) or engaged pilasters (p. 117) to give the feeling for the style without slavishly copying the complete order. Many Federal, and some earlier, houses were converted to the new style merely by adding columns, pilasters, and other motifs. Such modifications account for the great diversity seen in this style. And all these characteristics contributed to making the Greek Revival style the most popular in American history, lasting at least to the 1850s.

As in previous eras, the message of the new style was brought to the countryside by builder's manuals. One of the most widely read and adopted (if not copied) was Minard Lafever's *The Young Builder's General Instructor* (1829) and its successor *The Modern Builder's Guide* (1833). In time, however, some of the style's constraints came to be seen as too limiting. Its necessary rectangularity combined with its stark formality eventually led to a strong reaction in the opposite direction — to an architecture of fanciful details and functional plan that drew on the picturesque countryside of England.

In the Gothic Mode

By the 1840s America had spent over a century working out the implications of one classical style after another and now felt ready for a change from such formality, restraint, and ponderousness. It was time to give up the temple tradition and develop something entirely new and different. That something — the Gothic mode — was indeed different, almost the antithesis of the classical; but it certainly was not new. America had had over a century of experience with the Gothic. All its houses of the seventeenth century and many up to 1750 were true descendents of medieval Gothic architecture of northern Europe. The "new" Gothic of the 1840s and 1850s was a revival of northern Europe's age-old indigenous style.

The most obvious characteristic of Gothic architecture is the use of the pointed arch. The style's more basic and distinguishing feature, however, is the fact that its form derived from its structure. Buttresses, piers, vaults, and arches are not only its structural skeleton but also its visible and final effect, without classical or formal detail. This accounts for the similarity between the Dutch houses of Columbia County and the later Gothic Revival houses and churches. Both have exposed structural members on the inside and high gabled roofs like their common ancestors in Europe. This emphasis on natural materials honestly expressed is a legacy that continues today in contemporary architecture.

The Gothic Revival in America dates from 1799 when a newly arrived Englishman named Benjamin Latrobe, best-known for his design for the city of Washington and for the dome of the Capitol after the War of 1812, added some Gothic details to an otherwise classical house near Philadelphia. As the nineteenth century progressed, the Gothic became more popular as a decorative style, especially for churches, no doubt because of its association with the great cathedrals of Europe. The Gothic "cottage" style was another offshoot introduced by the architect Alexander Jackson Davis in the 1830s and popularized in Andrew Jackson Downing's publications on the subject during the 1840s and 1850s. Meadowbank (p. 132) is a product of this style and of an era of romantic ideals about the bucolic country life that spawned it. One of Downing's aesthetic tenets was that a country house should be of natural material with natural surfaces and colors. The frequent use of exterior vertical board and batten siding more "honestly" expressed the verticality of the interior structure, as in the case of Meadowbank. The somber brown earth color of St. John's Church in Stockport (p. 133), surrounded by compatibly vertical trees, expresses this ideal of harmony with nature. Indeed the popularity of this concept of man's relationship to nature imbues both the arts and architecture in America at this time. The Hudson River school of landscape painting was founded on this same inspiration.

The Gothic Revival as practiced in architecture prior to the 1840s was a romantic style created for its visual effect without strict conformity to its medieval antecedents. This began to change, however, under the influence of Richard Upjohn (1802–78). Upjohn's first important commission as an architect — and the one for which he is best known — was Trinity Church in New York City, begun in 1839. Trinty Church set a new standard of Gothic style, more clearly related to the original principles of Gothic architecture. The success of this design established Upjohn's Gothic as *the* style for Episcopal (and other) churches across the country. Many parishes in upstate New York applied to Upjohn for plans for modest structures in keeping with their even more modest budgets. (The New York City Trinity Corporation sometimes helped these parishes out.) Financial constraint, plus the architect's natural tendency to avoid superfluous details, resulted in churches that relied on admirable proportions to carry the beauty of their modest design. Upjohn designed three churches in Columbia County in the 1850s. St. Paul's in Kinderhook

(1852) (p. 134) is closely related to a drawing from the architect's book, *Upjohn's Rural Architecture* (1852). St. John's in the Wilderness in Copake (1852) (p. 134) is as simple as a church can be yet is pleasing and dignified. St. Luke's in Clermont (1859) (p. 135) is small but finished with picturesque details that reveal the influence of Upjohn's son, Richard M. Upjohn. Christ Church in Hudson (p. 135), although designed by the New York architect William G. Harison (1854–1857), clearly owes its inspiration to Upjohn.

After the 1850s, the Gothic Revival underwent a third change, this time to a variation on the original called High Victorian Gothic. The impetus for this shift came from the writings of John Ruskin who, in *Seven Lamps of Architecture* (1849), discussed many of the ideals of architecture. He drew especially on the early Gothic architecture of northern Italy, in which he emphasized such features as truthful materials, simple, grand massing, bold and irregular silhouettes, and hand-crafted materials. His influence, and that of others, produced a variation on the Gothic noted for the use of multiple colors in stone and brick, slate roofing, tile and wood trim, irregular and bold silhouettes, carving, and sometimes, ornate cast ironwork. One of the best surviving examples of this style in Columbia County is the Valatie Presbyterian Church built in 1877–78 (p. 135). At the time of its erection it was described in a county history book as "one of the handsomest in the country . . . a brick structure trimmed with blue limestone . . . designed after an old German cathedral." The last assertion is not strictly correct but does suggest the common Gothic basis for both.

As had happened once before in the eighteenth century, the Gothic mode went out of style in this area after its revival and fashion reverted to styles directly or indirectly inspired by classical forms. Styles of architecture, however, like most fashions are continually reborn in new guises. The Gothic returned yet again in the first decades of the twentieth century under the name of Neo-Gothic to grace the design of churches and colleges throughout the country and will, no doubt, be seen again.

The Italianate Style
Immediately following the Gothic style was one derived from the country villas of Italy. These houses

23

usually had a cupola on the roof which, though mainly decorative, gave a panoramic view of the countryside. Another version was an asymmetrical villa with an attached tower inspired by Italian Romanesque bell towers. This Italian style architecture became popular in England about 1800. In part it had been inspired by English travel accounts and drawings of the Italian countryside, but equally important was the influence of the French masters of the seventeenth century, Nicolas Poussin and Claude Lorrain, whose widely collected landscapes of Italy had depicted such villas. By the 1840s the style became popular in America and houses in one variant or another of the Italian villa were built over the next twenty years.

Much of the Italian flavor of these houses comes from their characteristically prominent eaves supported by heavy brackets, low sloping roofs, and verandas. These qualities also gave the houses a picturesque aspect, which, during this romantic era in American culture, was much desired. This picturesque aesthetic is evident in the asymmetrical design of the Reynolds house of 1856 in Kinderhook (p. 137) with its irregular outline created by a tall tower and blocks of different heights on either side. Asymmetry in the size of features or variations in their design also created a sense of the unexpected, adding mystery and a touch of the romantic.

Closely related in style if not structural form to the Italian villa house is the eight-sided house invented by Orson Squire Fowler (1809–87). This man had had a remarkably varied and successful career in the fields of phrenology, temperance, abolition, self-improvement, etc. A concern for the improvement of humanity led him to invent the octagon house as *A Home for All, or a New, Cheap, Convenient and Superior Mode of Building,* as he stated in the title of his book in 1848. The basis for the octagonal house was philosophical as well as practical: it most closely approximated a circle (nature's most beautiful and perfect shape, said Fowler), and it had less exterior wall exposure for interior space than other forms (hence less heat loss). In the 1850s and 1860s a considerable number of octagon houses were built in the United States. About three hundred survive today, of which three are in Columbia County (p. 146).

Architecture of the Second Empire
Named for the reign of Napoleon III (1852–70), the Second Empire style is characterized by tall, often curved, mansard roofs. This roof type had the advantage of making useful space of otherwise wasted attic space; and, in addition, the high roof gave an appearance of dignity and formality that enhanced otherwise plain structures.

The style began in France, became popular in England in the 1850s, and soon was in vogue in the United States. The imposing quality of the Second Empire style led to frequent use of it for large public buildings. The present New York capitol building was originally designed in this style. In Columbia County it was used for the most expensive houses of the 1860s and 1870s as well as for some more modest dwellings (p. 141). Italianate houses with flattish roofs were easily "updated" by the addition of a high mansard roof. The Waterbury house in Hudson (p. 147) is especially distinguished as the only example of that product of the Industrial Revolution — a house with a cast iron facade.

The last part of the nineteenth century witnessed an accelerated variety of architectural styles too numerous to describe in detail. Some, like the "stick" style, are indigenously American, while others, like the Queen Anne style, are clearly of English origin. Among these styles are Eastlake (similar to "stick" style), High Victorian Gothic (derived from the Gothic Revival), Shingle (for its siding), Richardson Romanesque (adopted from architect H. H. Richardson's designs), Colonial Revival (we have come full circle), Elizabethan Revival, and Academic Revival (a return to classicism).

Not until nearly the beginning of the twentieth century did American architecture make a fundamental change away from historically inspired styles. H. H. Richardson had initiated a change away from the traditional emphasis on style to an emphasis on function. Louis Sullivan, and then his student Frank Lloyd Wright, pursued this direction and in so doing changed the mainstream of architecture in America. In retrospect the turn of the century marks a watershed in American architecture (and art also) distinguished by a basic change in orientation from architectural design as a stylistic monument to an era to design as a response to human needs and the natural setting.

It took generations before new experiences reshaped Old World ways of life. In what was to become Columbia County, the white settlers of the seventeenth and eighteenth centuries were European — not Americans. In the wilderness, they cleared space for farms and roads. They built houses like those their parents or grandparents had known in the Netherlands or in England. From what art and architecture remain it is clear that, before the Revolution, the Dutch and English who settled Columbia County lived in a manner closely related to their European origins.

In the colonial period Columbia County was a part of Albany County. The earliest settlers were Dutch families from the city of Albany who undertook farming and milling along the streams that flowed into the Hudson River. Beginning sporadically about 1650, they acquired title to land in this area and began farms and settlements. Despite the fact that from 1664 on New York was under British rule, the Dutch maintained their traditional ways almost until the eve of the Revolution. After New Englanders began settling eastern Columbia County in the 1740s, a major cultural change began. Georgian influence, which had been present in New York City for fifty years, began to make itself felt. A third major influence on settlement during this period was the establishment of the Livingston Manor in the southern half of the county. The Livingston family brought a large migration of German Palatines to the region, established an iron industry, and influenced politics far beyond the bounds of their manor. The American Revolution brought to a natural end the European traditions of the region's residents. It gave them (at least most of them) an overriding common bond and a new identity as Americans with personal and collective responsibility for their own destiny.

I
In the European Tradition
ca. 1650–1783

The Land and the People

The earliest settlement of what later became Columbia County was affected by three types of land-ownership and government. In the south was the manorial system (Livingston Manor, established 1715), where certain legal and governmental privileges were vested in a single landowning family who rented land to tenants. In the central (Claverack) area of the county the Van Rensselaer family owned another large tract (since 1649); the family rented to tenants, but legal and governmental privileges were held by the Albany County government. The third and northern section of the county (Kinderhook) consisted of individually owned tracts; and in 1686 the governor granted the privileges of town government to the freeholders, who modeled their practices after the towns of Long Island. These three forms of land tenure and authority affected the settlement of Columbia County through the eighteenth century.

Although long considered the oldest existing house in Columbia County, the dates of its erection and alterations are in doubt. Abraham Staats, the progenitor of a large upper Hudson valley family, came from Holland to New Amsterdam in 1642 as a surgeon general in the employ of the Dutch West India Company. By 1655 he had moved to Albany where he was in the fur trade. By 1661 he owned the bowery at Stockport farmed by a tenant, Jan Andriessen. In July 1664 the house was burned and the tenant found dead in the house. Jeremias Van Rensselaer, Director of the Rensselaerwyck colony, reported that the fire had been set by two Indians acting under orders from the English. Thus the English effort to take over New Netherlands touched Columbia County.

Once under English rule, the Dutch had to reestablish their claims to the land, and in 1667 Abraham Staats acquired the first patent for the land on which the house is situated. From about that time, he may have been in residence at this place. His descendants occupied the house at least until the last half of the eighteenth century.

Although it is not possible to tell if the massive foundation and walls remain from the pre-1664 building, what early woodwork survives in the house is characteristic of Dutch houses of the first half of the eighteenth century or earlier. The present roof is not original but dates from the late nineteenth century. A small one-and-a-half-story brick wing was torn down by the present owner some years ago because it was in disrepair. In the process a very large earthenware jar and an earthenware roof tile were found, suggesting that either or both sections once had a pantile roof. An earthenware date stone from the brick wing is inscribed *S S* with the date of erection, 1769.

Abraham Staats house (ca. 1660s or later).
North side of Stockport Creek
near Hudson River, Stockport.

Robert Livingston (1718), oil on canvas, 51½" × 40", "Aetatis sue" limner. Private collection.

Like most early eighteenth-century New York portraits, this one is based on an English mezzotint — in this case, the 1715 engraved portrait of Nicholas Rowe. In posture, position of hands and head, costume, and background, the two are nearly identical. In American painting, however, the robe is an unusual costume and relates to Robert Livingston's career as attorney and provincial official.

The painter of this portrait is believed to be the unidentified "Aetatis Sue" limner — whose title is derived from his distinctive manner and style of inscribing his portraits to indicate the age of the sitter and the date of the painting. This painter is sometimes called the Schuyler limner because he painted several members of the Schuyler family. The "Aetatis Sue" limner worked in the Albany region on and off between 1715 and 1725. Robert Livingston's portrait is the first dated painting in Columbia County, a fact that complements the importance of the man himself.

The first Robert Livingston (1654–1728) was born in Scotland, the son of a dynamic Protestant minister and descended from an old and titled Scottish family. Religious turmoil caused his immediate family to be dispersed, and young Robert was raised and educated in the Netherlands. He emigrated to the New World in 1673, and within a year and a half was in Albany, attracted there by the flourishing fur trade. A year later he was appointed Secretary to the Board of Indian Commissioners. Since the English then controled Dutch New York, part of Robert Livingston's success resulted from his Anglo-Dutch background, which gave him a linguistic and cultural advantage not available to others in Albany. In 1679 he married Alida Schuyler Van Rensselaer, the young widow of Nicholas Van Rensselaer. After an abortive attempt to acquire a large portion of the lands in Rensselaerwyck, he purchased tracts of land amounting to 160,000 acres south of Albany at the Roeloff Janssen kill (1683) and at Taghkanic (1685) from the Indians. As it turned out, these "extravagant grants" of land were difficult to settle. As early as 1694, he sold two tracts of land comprising 1200 and 600 acres to his colleague Dirck Wessel Ten Broeck. Otherwise, tenant farmers were encouraged to settle there. In 1710 Livingston sold 6000 acres to Queen Anne for the use of the British government. Although British hopes for profitable pitch-tar manufacture on this acreage met with failure, the settlement of approximately eight hundred Palatines on the tract improved the prospects for the development of Livingston's lands. In 1715, the Manor of Livingston was erected. In his will Robert Livingston bequeathed to his eldest surviving son, Philip (1686–1749), the lordship of the manor. Philip's son, Robert, Jr. (1708–90), was the third and last lord. By the mid-eighteenth century manor lands were broken up either by sale or by devise to numerous Livingston heirs. This practice had originated with the first Robert, who bequeathed more than 11,000 acres southwest of the Roeloff Jansen kill (the present Town of Clermont) to his second youngest son, Robert (1688–1775), who built the house Clermont (see p. 48).

The Palatine emigration of 1710 was the largest mass influx of people during the colonial period. In 1709 the Palatines, representing a mix of Lutherans, Calvinists, Catholics, Mennonites, and other religious sects, left the Rhineland for England. They were driven not by religious persecution but by repeated deprivations caused by the Thirty Years War, oppressive taxation by the German princes, and finally, by the unusually severe winter of 1708–09, which killed plants, animals, and people and froze the edge of the sea solid. The Palatines, who had first received permission to emigrate to England, presented a massive problem to the British, who resolved it by turning them into a labor force to manufacture tar in the colonies; and at the end of the contract, each would become the owner of a forty-acre farm lot. Naval stores, like tall ship masts and tar, were essentials for shipbuilding; and a good source was the pitch pine forests on the Livingston Manor lands in New York. The British plan would both give them an entree into the profitable European market and solve the Palatine problem.

After being confined on ship board for nearly six months (From November to April they drifted in the English Channel waiting for better weather), in June 1710, about 3000 Palatines arrived at New York City, where they were quarantined at the outskirts of the city until their many diseases were cured. It was not until October that they were transported to a 6000-acre tract in the upper Hudson River valley that Robert Livingston had sold to Queen Anne for this purpose. Over 1200 persons — 342 families — began the villages of Hunterstown, Queensbury, Annsbury, and Haysbury at the East Camp (today's Germantown). Each person was assigned a lot and built a cottage from rough logs chinked with mud. No vestige of these settlements has survived, and even their exact locations are uncertain. Livingston contracted to supply bread and beer and to distribute other food and supplies sent from New York. At this time Gover-

Simon Rockefeller house/tavern (ca. 1755, later additions). County Route 8, Germantown.

nor Hunter and other colonial officials began to mismanage the venture. For example, the food and tools supplied were inadequate for the needs of the Palatines; further, proper instruction and supervision in the tar manufacturing process was not provided. In addition, the Palatines apparently did not find the work congenial, since they were, after all, farmers and vine-dressers. As a consequence, in 1712 the East Camp population dispersed, with about a quarter of them going to Schoharie and most of the remainder settling on the Livingston Manor lands and in nearby Dutchess County.

Because of the failure of this experiment New York gained a poor reputation among future German immigrants, who thereafter settled in other colonies such as North Carolina, New Jersey, and especially in Pennsylvania. A few, however, continued to come to New York. One of these was Diell Rockenfeller [sic] (1695–1769) of Eldschied, Westerwald, Germany, who came with his wife, Anna, and three of their children to the East Camp in 1733. He began by leasing a farm and eventually he built a house and a sawmill (1751), and maintained

a store there. It is said that at the time of his death he owned one-sixth of the town or 1000 acres. He willed his own house to his eldest son Philip. His son Simon was bequeathed land he was already using, so it may be that Simon's house was built well before the date of his father's 1769 will, perhaps around the time of his first marriage in 1754.

At an intersection of roads just east of the present village of Germantown, Simon Rockefeller built, sometime in the mid-eighteenth century, a house in the form of a one-and-a-half-story stone dwelling of two rooms, a typical house for this area and period.

Near the turn of the century the house became a tavern and was considerably expanded by doubling its size to the east or right side and increasing the height of the whole structure to two stories. A porch was added on both levels and extended across the entire front of the building, resulting in an expansive and functional tavern structure. It is probably the largest and earliest surviving tavern in Columbia County. In recent years it has been used as a multi-family dwelling.

Johannes Ten Broeck
(1720) oil on canvas, 39½" × 46½",
inscribed "Etat⁵. Sue. 37. 1720," "Aetatis sue" limner.
Courtesy of the Philadelphia Museum of Art

Catryna Van Rensselaer Ten Broeck
(1720) oil on canvas, 39½" × 46½",
inscribed "Etat⁵. Suae. 29. 1720," "Aetatis sue" limner.
Courtesy the Philadelphia Museum of Art

Johannes Ten Broeck (1683–1768) was the second son of one of Albany County's largest land owners in the late seventeenth century. Dirck Wessels Ten Broeck (1638–1717), along with other prominent Albanians, purchased large tracts at Saratoga and the Westonhook patent in eastern Columbia County and western Massachusetts from the Indians and, with Evert Luycasse Backer, tracts at Kinderhook. He also owned 1800 acres within Livingston Manor, lands purchased from Robert Livingston in 1694. His son Johannes inherited houses and lots in Albany and at Kinderhook, the family merchant stores at Albany, and lands along Kinderhook Creek, which ran into the Westonhook patent. Johannes, however, was an absentee landlord, preferring to live in Albany, and after 1743 in New Brunswick, New Jersey.

Johannes' wife Catryna (1691–1770) was also from an absentee-landlord family. Her father Hendrick Van Rensselaer (1667–1740) had been given large tracts of land at Greenbush and Claverack in 1704 by his brother Kiliaen, Lord of the Manor of Rensselaerwyck. Although Johannes and Catryna Ten Broeck never lived in Columbia County, they and their absentee relatives exerted a major influence on subsequent settlement and politics of the area for generations by virtue of their vast land holdings. Later in the eighteenth century major disputes arose over both the Massachusetts–New York border and the titles to these eastern lands. The border area of Columbia County was claimed by numerous individuals. The ill-defined Westonhook patent, located along the Green and Housatonic Rivers, was a particular point of contention. Johannes and Catryna's son, Cornelis Ten Broeck (1717–66) was killed in a skirmish over these claims.

The portraits of Johannes and Catryna Ten Broeck are typical of those done in the Hudson valley at this period. The painter of these two portraits is the unidentified Aetatis Sue limner whose works are characterized by the dramatically painted folds of women's garments and the distinctive glove held and worn by gentlemen.

Paintings were not restricted to the households of major landowning Hudson valley families like the Livingstons and Ten Broecks. Properous middle-class families like the Van Alstynes were established there and enjoyed some of the luxuries of their Hudson River patrician neighbors. Thomas (1688–1764/5) and Marietje (1695–after 1765) Van Alstyne were not known for civic leadership in county or provincial affairs, nor had they intermarried with more prominent families. Perhaps the freeheld land governed in common by the proprietors of the town of Kinderhook (established 1686) lay behind the apparent success of these people.

Thomas' grandfather, Jan Martense, one of Kinderhook's earliest settlers, had lived in Albany during the 1650s and 1660s. In 1671 he purchased large tracts of land along Kinderhook Creek. Lambert Janse Van Alstyne, one of his sons, inherited 670 acres of this tract on the east side of the creek.

This in turn was inherited by Lambert's oldest son, Thomas, by 1714. In 1718 Thomas married Marietje Van Alen, a daughter of Willem Van Alen, who was both a farmer and a sloop captain, residing across the river at Bethlehem. Typical of many young Dutchmen, Thomas did not marry until after he had established himself financially. Besides farming, Van Alstyne operated a yacht carrying farm produce and goods on the river, ran a brewery and a sawmill, and engaged in some real estate speculation. Around the middle of the eighteenth century he was the wealthiest man in Kinderhook. His life covered seventy-seven years — a span that saw the beginnings of Columbia County wrested from the wilderness to the eve of the Revolution. It was his heirs who sold a stone house on prime creekside land in 1787 to Peter Van Ness. Van Ness built there a large Federal house, later renamed Lindenwald, the home of Martin Van Buren *(see p. 136)*.

Thomas Van Alstyne
Marietje Van Alen Van Alstyne
Both oil on canvas, 39¼″ × 30″,
"Aetatis Sue" limner.
Courtesy New-York Historical
Society, New York City.
Gift of Brig.-Gen. and Mrs.
John Ross Delafield, 1930.

Catherine Van Alstyne, inscribed "Aged 13 month 1732,"
oil on canvas, 39³/₁₆″ × 29⅞″,
Wendell limner.
Courtesy Albany Institute of History and Art.
Gift of Mrs. Ledyard Cogswell, Jr.

This portrait was one of six to eight family pictures that decorated the walls of Thomas and Marietje Van Alstyne's home near Kinderhook. Thomas' will (dated 1760) mentions portraits of each of his three sons, but the portraits of himself and his wife and daughter are grouped with "household goods." Although none of the portraits of other children are known to survive, portraits of his other two daughters seem likely to have been made. Family paintings like these were given important places in Dutch households.

The Wendell limner, identified through three known portraits of members of Albany's Wendell family, is known to have painted a small number of portraits of other upper Hudson valley residents. Since this portrait's inscription is in English, rather than Dutch or Latin, it is likely that the painter was of English extraction. The Wendell limner often gave special attention to patterned silks and brocades, luxuries in the colonial period.

The Dominance of Dutch Culture

The early settlers of Columbia County maintained their Dutch culture in both architecture and furnishings. Their houses were derived directly from the old-country medieval prototypes common in northern Europe. Houses very similar to the Luykas Van Alen house can still be found in Holland today.

The Dutch fondness for numerous paintings also carried over to the New World, resulting in the first sustained period of American painting. A dozen or more limners painted for the prosperous residents along the Hudson River from New York to Albany. Today more than three hundred of these paintings, executed between 1700 and 1750 in colonial New York, still survive as reminders of this first "school" of artists in America.

The Dutch attraction to material wealth and their successful pursuit of it have left us a rich heritage of material culture from the colonial period.

Luykas Van Alen house (1737). Route 9H, Kinderhook.

Lourens Van Alen and his father-in-law, Evert Luycasse Backer, were among the earliest land purchasers at Kinderhook. When Evert Luycasse died about 1700, the nine children of Lourens and Elbertje, Evert's only daughter, became heir to about 10,000 acres of land. Lourens himself continued to purchase land and at the time of his death in 1714, the nine children inherited approximately another 10,000 acres. All this property, including numerous parcels along Kinderhook Creek, as well as a large tract next to the river, was divided equally among them in 1714. Johannes, as the eldest son, inherited Lourens' homestead, where Luykas had lived with his father. Consequently, Luykas purchased, prior to his marriage in 1726, nearby land where he built his house in 1737. The house was occupied by seven generations of this family and in 1964 was given to Columbia County Historical Society, which

has undertaken an extensive restoration program to preserve the present thirty-three acres and the house as a museum of Dutch life in the mid-eighteenth century.

Architecturally the Van Alen house is one of fewer than a dozen of its type that have survived intact from the early eighteenth century. Its style is distinguished by parapet gables rising about its steeply pitched roof. Such houses, however, were not built by the first settlers. Only after two or three generations had cleared the wilderness, established local government and churches, and made their farms profitable, did the community's most successful landowners, farmers, and merchants built substantial homes adorned with medieval northern European elegance. Other houses of similar style survive in Kinderhook, Claverack, and Greenport.

Fireplace, Luykas Van Alen house.

Framing and window, Luykas Van Alen house.

Each room has its own open fireplace. The chimneys are built on a heavy wooden framework of beams in the ceiling and are secured to the wall in mortise-and-tenon fashion. Each room has its own entry and is part of an add-on floor plan, wherein rooms are arranged in a row, one after another.

Smooth, planed ceiling beams and knee braces were details specified in early building contracts. Transom and casement windows and Dutch half-doors were built into the vertical framing of the house.

Besides fur traders and merchants, specialized craftsmen like Martin Vosburgh, "carpenter of Kinderhook," worked in the Dutch communities along the upper Hudson.

Masonry and iron wall anchors,
Luykas Van Alen house.

Functional elements of Dutch houses included decorative iron wall anchors that secured heavy interior framing to the brick exterior in which the bond forms an attractive pattern.

Although it is not known who built this house for Luykas Van Alen, local records do show that Caspar Roush was a mason living at Kinderhook during the 1720s and 1730s. Housewrights like Roush worked in the medieval building tradition of the Netherlands until the middle of the eighteenth century.

The Gansevoort limner is identified by the portraits he made of members of the Gansevoort family of Albany. Altogether about eighteen portraits of the 1730s and 1740s have been attributed to this painter. Of these, several have been handed down with the tradition that they were painted by Pieter Vanderlyn (1687–1778), a native of the Netherlands, who came to New York City around 1718 and to Kingston in 1722. He married there Gertruy Vas, the daughter of the Dutch domine at Kingston. Most of his life he lived at Kingston although during the 1730s he resided in Albany.

In the twentieth century, many early New York paintings were incorrectly attributed to Vanderlyn because a knowledge of his name survived while knowledge of his work did not. Researchers have now found the names of a dozen or so limners, and their task is to identify each limner with his surviving work. A study by Mary Black indicates that the Gansevoort limner is indeed Pieter Vanderlyn.

This limner's style differs from that of the Aetatis Sue limner and Duyckinck family limners: although he depended, as they did, on mezzotint sources for ideas, he did not copy them. He depicted elegance by rendering contemporary American fashion rather than the elegantly flowing drapery of the English mezzotints. In general this limner's use of outlined figures filled in with thinly painted areas of color conforms with the practice of non-academic painters.

Of six Van Alen brothers, only two — Pieter and Stephanus — had daughters who would have been between ten and twenty years old in the early 1730s. Since the age of the girls cannot readily be determined from their portraits, it is not possible to identify them with certainty. Both Pieter and Stephanus Van Alen lived along the Kinderhook Creek not far from their brother, Luykas Van Alen. Family wills and other documents listing paintings show that the Van Alens shared the enthusiasm of other New York Dutch for portraits and other paintings.

Elizabeth Van Brugh (1712–46) was the daughter of Pieter Van Brugh, a mayor of Albany. When she married her first cousin Hendrick Van Rensselaer (1712–93) in 1735, they took up residence at Claverack, the large tract of land Hendrick's father had received in 1704 as a gift from his brother Kiliaen, lord of the manor of Rensselaerwyck. Here the couple raised their children, and Hendrick kept stores for Claverack residents, supplying them with a variety of goods usually paid for with farm produce and, occasionally, cash. In 1743, Governor Clinton appointed Hendrick Captain of the Militia of Foot at Claverack.

Although it is likely that Hendrick had his portrait painted, as was customary among the well-to-do-Albany Dutch, it has not been found. This portrait of Elizabeth descended in the family with the information that it was painted before her marriage. Because of similarities to other portraits painted by him during this time, it is attributed to Gerardus Duyckinck (1695–1746), one of a New York family whose members had been painters for several generations. The attribution to him is further strengthened by the fact that Gerardus Duyckinck married Johanna Van Brugh, Elizabeth's sister. Duyckinck and his wife were baptismal witnesses for two of Hendrick's and Elizabeth's children. These visits and possibly others, which are suggested by transactions recorded in Hendrick's account books for his stores at Claverack and Schenectady, suggest he might have influenced the work of other painters in Albany County during the late 1730s. Like the Aetatis Sue limner, Duyckinck based his poses on English mezzotint prints of the time (themselves copies of oil portraits by leading contemporary English painters). In portraits of the 1730s, however, a directness and accuracy of detail reflected the influence of an earlier painting style of seventeenth-century England and the Netherlands.

Elizabeth Van Brugh
(Mrs. Hendrick) Van Rensselaer (ca. 1730),
oil on canvas, 45½" × 36¼",
attributed to Gerardus Duyckinck.
Courtesy The New-York Historical Society,
New York City,
Gift of Duncan Sill, 1924.

The Rise of English Taste

The advent of New Englanders and English colonial culture into what is now Columbia County dates from the mid-eighteenth century. Although the French and Indian Wars only slightly touched the county, they did result in the first significant alteration to the prevailing Dutch culture in the upper Hudson valley. In the area that was to become Columbia County, New Englanders came first as soldiers crossing the Berkshires en route to garrisons at Albany. English soldiers and a barage of English, Irish, and Scottish merchants came up the river, and many of them remained. The effect of these migrations was a very gradual acceptance of English culture. In the 1760s the local Dutch adapted the gambrel roof (two slants to a side). The style had been popular in lower New York since the late seventeenth century and before that in New England where it originated. It is not, as commonly believed, indicative of a true Dutch house. In Columbia County the gambrel roof form was used by persons of Dutch, English, and New England cultures from the 1760s through the 1790s.

Johannes L. Van Alen house (ca. 1760s). Schoolhouse Road, Stuyvesant.

Spacious gambrel-roof houses, usually with a central hall and one or two rooms on either side, became fashionable in what is now Columbia County in the 1760s. The room arrangement, plastered and corniced ceilings, paneled walls over jambed fireplaces, and second-floor bedrooms are all akin to Georgian features found elsewhere in the colonies and represent an abrupt departure from the features of true Dutch homes. On the exterior, sidelights, not heavy framework, flank the Dutch door. A Palladian-inspired window replaces the transom light. Most of the original paneled windows and doors, raised panel wainscot, paneled stairway, flooring, joists, and cornices survive in this house. One, and possibly two, paneled fireplace walls have long since been removed, though parts survive. During a restoration in the 1960s, much Victorian ornamentation was removed leaving the structure nearer its original form.

Johannes L. Van Alen (1730–1804) was the second son of Luykas Van Alen. His farm and house are on lands originally bought by his grandfather *(see p. 33).* He married Christina Van Dyck in 1761 and raised nine children here, including Elizabeth *(see p. 54)* who married Peter Van Schaack in 1789.

Barn, Johannes L. Van Alen farm.

Unlike most farms, this one is little changed from its early days. Two Dutch barns survive from the eighteenth century. This one, with its widely sloping roof and centered doorway in the gable end, is especially characteristic of New York Dutch barns. Space in the center aisle was used for flailing and winnowing wheat and for wagon storage. The side aisles accommodated animals stalls and pens, as well as feeding troughs.

One of the most appealing early farms in Columbia County is the Ten Broeck Bowery. Situated at the foot of an escarpment, it overlooks the fields bordering the Roeloff Jansens' kill. A walk down the dirt road from the family burial ground, past the barns and between the huge locust trees before the house is as close to an eighteenth-century experience as one can get in Columbia County.

The house is as appealing as the grounds. It was built by the grandson and namesake of the first Ten Broeck to settle in the county. The bowery along the Roeloff Jansen kill was a tract of 2000 acres purchased in 1694 from Robert Livingston by Dirck Wessels Ten Broeck, who was a kind of lieutenant or business manager on the Livingston manor. Like most surviving houses built in the 1760s, it has a gambrel roof, and its rooms are arranged on either side of a central hall. The height of the house is unusual, being a full two stories high with a spacious attic. Like all brick structures up to this time, it is laid in Dutch bond (*see p. 35*). It is additionally ornamented by the date 1762 in brick between the upstairs front windows and by a series of three diamond patterns on the north gable end. The interior includes an original panel wall on the second floor and part of another such wall.

Extending to the rear of the main section is an early one-room house believed to date from 1736. (Parts of a dated panel were once found in this room) With its large beams joined to wall posts by knee braces and framed to hold the chimney of an open fireplace, it is evident that this earlier house was of the true Dutch type similar to the Luykas Van Alen House (*p. 36*) but more modest in size.

*View of the Ten Broeck Bowery at Clermont
(late eighteenth century), paper cutout,
Albertina Ten Broeck Sanders.
Reproduced from the* Ten Broeck Family Genealogy, *1899.*

This unique document shows the appearance of a Dutch farm in the later part of the eighteenth century. The house and well remain intact, but the large Dutch barn similar to the barn on *p. 39* is gone, replaced by somewhat later barns.

In the family genealogy this cutout view, done in the last quarter of the eighteenth century, is identified as the Ten Broeck homestead that preceded the Bowery *(see p. 40)*. Since a large sailing vessel is illustrated, the house is more likely to be the one built on that part of Dirck Wessel Ten Broeck's purchase from the first Robert Livingston that was on the river.

Sheep and boat and wellsweep are charming details that add interest to this depiction of colonial life along the Hudson.

*View of Bowery
at Germantown,
paper cutout.
Albertina Ten
Broeck Sanders
Reproduced from*
Ten Broeck Family
Genealogy, *1899.*

*Paneled chimney breast, John Bay house (ca. 1760s).
Route 23, Claverack.*

The center part of this over-mantel paneling is a sophisticated example of Georgian joinery. Many houses built between 1760 and 1790 in the upper Hudson River valley had an entire end of the room covered by this type of raised paneling, which surrounded a fireplace in the center with cupboards on either side. As fashions changed, these walls were removed. This one survived on the second floor of John Bay's gambrel-roofed house in the hamlet of Claverack. It is probably the finest example of a paneled wall still to be seen in Columbia County.

The Reformed Protestant Dutch Church
(1767, plus later additions). Route 9H, Claverack.

This second structure of the Dutch congregation at Claverack replaced a more primitive building constructed around 1727. When the second minister, Dom. Johannes C. Fryenmoet began his service at Claverack in 1756, he began to urge the construction of a new edifice. In early 1767 John Van Rensselaer, then proprietor of most of the land in Claverack, deeded the congregation land for a new church and parsonage. This meant a change of location, a move unpopular with many parishioners. When the second church was built, it was identified as the Van Rensselaer church. Indeed John Van Rensselaer had his own elevated and canopied pew — a fact that prompted one disgruntled parishioner to mutter a threat of taking an axe to the church and hewing it down. This, along with other disagreements related to title and border disputes, resulted in a schism in the church in 1770, with some members departing to form a new congregation in Hillsdale and Dom. Fryenmoet moving to Kinderhook. The lovely but luckless church had a lean period until the young Dom. John Gabriel Gebhard, fleeing the British in New York City, accepted a call to the Claverack church in 1776. He was the last minister called to America who was required to preach in the Dutch language. During his fifty-year pastorate the church prospered and continued to do so during the pastorate of his successor.

The year numerals are laid in the brickwork. The wings were added, probably between 1844 and 1859, with noteworthy sensitivity to the original style of the building. It is the oldest institutional building in the county.

Daniel Penfield Map of Claverack (1799) (detail).
Collection, Columbia County Historical Society.

The building committee of 1767 included Samuel Ten Broeck, whose father, Dirck Wessels Ten Broeck, had recently completed the Ten Broeck Bouwery. The Penfield map indicates that by 1799 the tower and belfry had been added.

The Argument with Massachusetts

In the colonial period settlement of the mountainous eastern region of Columbia County was a slow process complicated by conflicting land claims and an undetermined border between Massachusetts and New York. Three main routes between New England and the Hudson River crossed the county. From the 1660s onward, New Englanders used these roads that traversed Columbia County to bring farm produce to the Hudson River. Dutch interest in the eastern lands dates from 1684 when Dirck Wessels Ten Broeck, Pieter Schuyler, and others purchased lands along the Westonhook Creek (the Housatonic River in Massachusetts) from Westonhook Indians. A few Dutch families from Kinderhook and Claverack settled there in the early part of the eighteenth century. In the 1730s they complained to Boston authorities that New Englanders were encroaching on their lands. By the 1740s and 1750s, however, New Englanders were settling the western Berkshire foothills. Although they did not receive official authorization, the settlers organized effective town governments, which divided their lands (purchased from the Indians a second time) into lots and roads.

Since the boundary between Massachusetts and New York had not been established, whether Livingston and Claverack lands extended twenty or twenty-four miles east of the river was of momentous question. Claverack lands overlapped some of the region settled by the New Englanders. Furthermore, Claverack proprietor, John Van Rensselaer (1708–83), in connivance with Westonhook proprietors (including his son-in-law, Philip Schuyler), laid claim to all the lands east of Kinderhook Creek. The legality of this claim was tenuous.

Overriding colonial authorities, petitioners from Spencertown, New Canaan, Lebanon, New Britain, and Kinderhook appealed to the King, who in 1772 erected the Districts of Kinderhook and Kings. The lengthy border disputes were finally settled after several inter-colonial conferences in 1773, though the agreement was not made official until a 1787 act of Congress. The issue of land titles in the northeastern portions of Columbia County was not completely resolved until 1791 and 1793 when the state legislature passed acts conferring title to those who occupied the land in this area.

Saltbox (last half of the eighteenth century).
County Route 5, Canaan.

Repeating the Dutch experience of fifty to seventy-five years before, New England settlers from the east brought to the Columbia County region characteristic elements of their culture. Like the Dutch, they continued to build their homes in a style that had gone out of fashion in New England around the turn of the eighteenth century. The style they favored was a New England translation of medieval Elizabethan domestic architecture. Often regarded as an early and distinctly American form of domestic architecture, these clapboard houses developed in seventeenth century New England. Massive central chimneys served from three to five fireplaces and provided more efficient use of heat than Dutch and Georgian chimneys, located on outer walls. The interiors of these houses often had more elaborate details than their severe exteriors suggest. Several houses of this type survive in northeastern Columbia County.

Gravestone for Asa Douglass (1812),
unidentified stonecutter.
Town of Canaan.

*Gravestone of Nathaniel Gilbert (1787),
unidentified stonecutter. Town of Lebanon.*

New Englanders brought distinctive gravestone verses and designs with them as they settled on Columbia County land. Sculpture and poetry in stone have immortalized many settlers of the Kings District. The family of Nathaniel Gilbert (1723–87) likely commissioned this epitaph on his gravestone:

> *Beneath this stone in peaceful slumber lies*
> *Gilbert the just, benevolent, and wise*
> *This dust shall live, and its glad spirit join,*
> *And rise to life immortal and divine.*

The stonecutters' craft was not without its practical aspects. For example, Pliny Moor, of the Spencertown area, received this solicitation in 1787.

Sr, at your Request I have made two Pair of Grave Stones and Conveyed them to the meeting house at Spencer Town. I understand you have seen them and are Satisfied with the Performance: you wrote to me that you Did not Know that you Could Pay me so Soon as the Work was Done. I have waited a short time and would not have wrote to you now if the Exigency of my affairs had Not obliged me to it, being obliged to Borrow Money to Pay my Tax. the Price for the two Pair is five Dollars. if you would be so good as to send me the money by Simon Ford the Bearer of this Letter or at Least a part I should be much obliged to you and shall Remain your most humble Servant

Truman Powell*

Truman Powell was the son of one of the original settlers in Green River, in the present Town of Austerlitz. In his own will (dated 6 August 1805, registered 7 January 1806), he specified that ten or twelve dollars was to be spent for his own gravestone.

*The McLelland Collection of Pliny Moore Papers.

In 1750 a large group of New Englanders, many from Canaan, Connecticut, purchased from the Indians a six-mile tract along the upper Stoney Kill. Since there was a question as to whether or not it had been previously owned, settlement progressed erratically for fifteen years. About 1764 Asa Douglass (1739–1812), later Major Douglass, following other members of his family, settled at Canaan. His epitaph describes him as one of Canaan's first settlers. As an officer in the Revolution, he attained notoriety among the British for his ability to deal with Tories skulking in the woods.

By the 1760s men like Asa Douglass, in New Concord, New Britain, New Canaan, Spencertown, Green River, and Lebanon Springs, began to farm the long narrow valleys of Punsit and Wyomanock Creeks, Stoney Kill, and Green River. These quick mountain streams provided water power for numerous gristmills and sawmills in the eighteenth and nineteenth centuries. Agricultural skills acquired on rocky New England land aided the settlers of these hilly regions.

The Livingston Family: Clermont and the Manor

Ever since Robert Livingston, the first lord of the manor, divided his manor between two of his sons, two branches of the family remained predominant in county and provincial affairs. Their land encompassed the southern third of the county; within its bounds a number of significant events took place: the large Palatine settlement, eastern border disputes associated with the intrusion of New England settlers, and the establishment of New York's first ironworks. From Clermont and from the manor, prosperous members of this talented and aggressive family helped shape the colonial and revolutionary history of New York.

Margaret Beekman Livingston (ca. 1764), oil on canvas, 31¼" × 36", Thomas McIlworth. The Columbia County Historical Society. Gift of Mrs. Frank Washburn, 1937.

On a return voyage from business in Albany in July 1774, Treasurer of the Province Abraham Lott recorded a stop at Clermont in his travel journal. In the morning the wind had failed and the tide was against the sloop in which he was traveling. Anchoring the vessel about a mile below Clermont, Abraham Lott went to "the house of Judge Livingston and Dined there, . . . — I was received very kindly here and at half past 2, o'clock left the House when Mrs. Livingston presented me with four Chickens and Some Carrots."

The eleven sons and daughters of Judge Robert and Margaret Livingston (1724–1800) were prominent in New York's social and business life during the Revolution and the Federal Period. True to family tradition, they built stately homes, most of them on Dutchess County lands.

Thomas McIlworth appeared in New York City in 1757 and worked there for five years before moving northward to paint portraits at Clermont, Albany, and Schenectady. From there, he went to Montreal, where he seems to have died about 1770. His life before 1757 is unknown, but he appears to have had little or no formal training. His portraits suggest that he was influenced by the work of trained English-born artists who began to appear in New York about 1750.

The original (1730) house was built in the Georgian style and rebuilt in that same style around 1778. As it appears today, it has wings, added in 1802; a steep pitched roof, added in 1874; and an enlarged south wing begun in 1830 and completed by 1888.

The British devised a three-pronged attack through New York that would cut New England off from the southern colonies. General Burgoyne was to drive down the Champlain valley; General Vaughan was to sail a fleet up the Hudson; General St. Leger was to invade eastward through the Mohawk valley all to meet in Albany, thereby separating north and south. General Vaughan moved up the Hudson (burning Kingston, then the state capital), and moved toward Clermont, which he also burned just as Margaret Beekman Livingston fled with her family and belongings. Upon receiving word of the American victory at Saratoga, Vaughan retreated to New York.

In the spring of 1778, Margaret Livingston began plans to rebuild Clermont. In a letter to his brother John, her son Robert wrote

Mama left us this morning to return to Clare Mount where she has put up a hut & spent great part of last week — It made me extremely melancholy a day or two ago to see the ruins. I can hardly describe my sensations at seeing the top of the chimney over the hill, an object which always excited the most pleasing emotions as it was an earnest of the joys of that once social fire side . . . When I came down the hill I saw Mama in her garden, tending with solitary care those plants her hands had reared in happier times . . . She has no pleasure any where else, or in any conversation but the mode of rebuilding & improving this place. She wanders about like the gost that reluctantly quits the body which was once the vehicle of its joys. . . .

That fall she had devised her mode of rebuilding her house. She sent a letter to the new governor of New York, George Clinton, asking him to exempt soldiers from the local militia to help her rebuild her home. He granted her request, and Clermont was rebuilt on the same foundations (and possibly with the old walls) of the mansion that Robert, son of the first lord, had built in 1730. As rebuilt, the house apparently was similar, if not identical, to its former appearance. In 1796 Archibald or Alexander Robertson recorded its appearance before additions were added in the nineteenth century.

"Clermont, Seat of Mrs. Livingston, September 14, 1796," pen drawing on paper, 9" × 11½", (detail). Alexander Robertson or Archibald Robertson. Courtesy The New-York Historical Society, New York City.

The first lord's son Robert (1688–1775) received from his father a large section of land south of the Roeloff Jansen kill that subsequently became known as Clermont. It is said that this bequest was in gratitude for his son's discovering and frustrating an Indian incursion against the manor. In 1730 Robert of Clermont built a large Georgian mansion on a high bluff overlooking the river. It was the first of its type in the upper Hudson valley. His son Robert (1718–75), known as Robert the Judge, married (1742) Margaret Beekman, the daughter of Col. Henry Beekman, owner of large estates south of Clermont. When her father-in-law, her husband, and her own father all died within a year of each other, she retained Clermont as her home, although her son Robert *(see p. 60)* inherited the Clermont and Dutchess County lands. Then in October 1777 events came to a climax.

Clermont (ca. 1778;
later changes and additions).
Woods Road, Clermont.
Clermont State Historic Site,
New York State
Office of Parks
and Recreation.

49

Portraits of Philip and Christina Ten Broeck Livingston
(ca. 1771), oil on canvas, 50" × 40", attributed to
Abraham Delanoy. Courtesy Clermont State Historic Site,
New York State Office of Parks & Recreation

The Manor and Clermont were headquarters for the wide-ranging Livingstons. This Philip Livingston (1716–78), a second son of Philip, second lord of the manor, was a prominent New York City merchant, sometimes delegate to the New York provincial assembly, a representative to the Continental Congress, and one of New York's signers of the Declaration of Independence. His wife Christina (1718–1801) was the great-granddaughter of Dirck Wessels Ten Broeck, who first purchased the Bowery *(see p. 40).*

Abraham Delanoy (1742–ca. 1795), a native of New York City and kin to the Duyckinck family, went to England to study painting under Benjamin West. He returned to New York City where he worked between 1767 and 1771. In painting style, he is less accomplished than Gilbert Stuart *(see p. 60),* but his work exhibits style greater than the stereotyped portraits of Thomas McIlworth, who preceded him in New York.

Teviotdale (1774–75), the Walter Livingston house.
Livingston.

Teviotdale is especially interesting, not only for its fashionable late Georgian architecture, but also because its construction is better documented than any other house in the county. Records of the first owner, Walter Livingston, preserved at The New-York Historical Society, were recently the subject of an exhaustive study by Lynn Beebe of the New York State Office of Historic Preservation.

Walter Livingston (1740–97) was the sixth child of Robert, the last lord of the manor (1708–90), and at the age of nineteen he entered Cambridge University, one of only seven men in colonial New York to attend a great English University. In 1766 he led a band of forty men who dispersed the first major rebellion that arose out of land controversies between New England and New York *(see p. 11).* A year later he married Cornelia Schuyler and settled

50

in New Jersey. He was an attorney but also followed careers in politics, trade, and land investment. In 1773, Walter Livingston sold his New Jersey property and purchased a 498-acre tract of manor land from his father. The conveyance included a stipulation of £7 annual rent. His previous stay in England must have made him well-acquainted with current English fashions, for the house he subsequently had erected was quite in keeping with contemporary English taste — something of an anomaly in the stylistically conservative Hudson valley.

From George Sperling, a builder, he obtained two estimates for construction: one price for completing the building with its stone walls exposed and a second price for the same to be "finished with a hard finish in imitation of stone." According to his subsequent agreement with Sperling, he chose the more economical option. Even so, the house cost him nearly twice as much as he had anticipated (£1302 as opposed to the estimate of £700). At some later time, the exterior walls were finished with stucco ruled to imitate cut stone (ashlar), thus concealing the rough stone that may after all have been a traditionally provincial feature.

John O'Brien, a stone mason, began construction with the laying of the first foundation stone on April 5, 1774. Construction was rapid; Walter and Cornelia Livingston moved in on December 14, and by the following spring the house was essentially complete. Prevailing classical influences are suggested by the plans, which called for a front doorway of the "Taskan [Tuscan] type."

Besides the house, Livingston built thirteen dependencies, including a Dutch barn and a hay barrack. In 1778 he built a piazza and later (1795) bought materials for a "railing on the house," perhaps a balustrade on the roof. At the same time, he made calculations for the construction of two small "houses" and two "octogens," though no further evidence of these has come to light. An 1827 sketch of the house signed "J. F." (without doubt Julia Fulton, Robert and Harriet's daughter) shows the east wing and verandas on both the back and front of the house.

At the time of its construction Walter Livingston was becoming involved in the politics of revolution. He served on the New York Committees of Sixty (1774) and One Hundred (1775), and in 1777 he was elected to the New York State Assembly and served as its first speaker until 1779. The Continental Congress had appointed him as Deputy Commissary General of the Northern Department, serving under the command of Gen. Philip Schuyler. In October 1777, General Vaughan's mission up the Hudson prompted him to evacuate the house and remove its furnishings. After the war, he served in the Congress and Treasury and was one of the commissioners appointed to settle the New York–Massachusetts border disputes (see p. 44). All his public positions bespoke a capable political sense and strong financial abilities.

Walter Livingston died in 1797. One of his children, Harriet, who was raised in Chancellor Robert Livingston's household, married Robert Fulton (see p. 63) and local tradition closely associates the inventor of the steamboat with the history of the house.

David Van Schaack mansion (1774). Route 9, Kinderhook.

Patriots and Loyalists in the Revolution

During the Revolutionary period, the region that is now Columbia County was still part of Albany County and the scene of the most heated patriot and Tory conflicts. The border and land disputes of the preceding fifty years affected the attitudes of many residents of the region. Often — though not always — local residents supported the position opposite to that espoused by community leaders. Many who lived on Livingston Manor were Tory activists, opposing the views of the Livingston family. The opposite was true at Kinderhook, where locally prominent persons remained loyal to the King and the majority of the town was ardently patriotic and succeeded in overthrowing the loyalist leaders. On the other hand, it is not suprising that Kinderhook landowners failed to support Johannes and Henry Van Rensselaer and their young in-law Gen. Philip Schuyler, who had sought control of Kinderhook lands.

Tory and patriot activities among New Englanders defy such classification. Whether loyalist or patriot, remarkable cooperation cut the tradition division between the Dutch and English populace.

The county was not the scene of war activity as such, save for the burning of Clermont. However, the Great New England Road and the north–south highway between New York and Albany carried important travelers through the area.

Since the early eighteenth century the Van Schaack family had been prominent in the village of Kinderhook. Cornelis Van Schaack was a prosperous merchant, and three of his sons achieved distinction: David for the fine Georgian house he built, Peter for his political and legal acumen, and Henry for financial and political abilities. During the Revolution, they were the leading loyalists in Kinderhook. In the upper Hudson valley at that time political commitments were often based on family or community associations rather than on strong views on freedom from tyranny or allegiance to the crown. The Van Schaack's loyalist feeling came out in an embarrassing moment on the evening of October 22, 1777, when the British general John Burgoyne was entertained at David Van Schaack's house while he and his army were being escorted in captivity to Boston after their defeat at Saratoga. Toward the end of dinner David Van Schaack's niece Lydia, age four, felt it was her turn to propose a toast and blurted out in front of Burgoyne's American captors, "God save the King and all the Royal Family."

Abraham Lott, Treasurer of the Colony, passed through Kinderhook in 1774 and noted David Van Schaack's new house in his journal:

David Van Schaack has built him a house like a castle near the town. It is built of brick, two stories high, four rooms on a floor and a large hall through the middle of it, and is built in very elegant Taste.

A century later David's nephew Henry Cruger Van Schaack wrote a memoir about this house and its family in which he states that the house was built in 1774. The walls of the spacious lower hall, as he described, were originally covered with imported English landscape papering representing a hunting scene, and originally all the fireplaces, of which one fireplace still remains intact, were ornamented with delft scripture tiles. He described an iron fireback in the dining room fireplace ornamented with stars and the date 1789, the year in which David's brother Peter built his own house next door. He

Peter Van Schaack, engraving, after a portrait by Jonathan Trumbull. From Henry C. Van Schaack's The Life of Peter Van Schaack *(1842).*

went on to say that David had originally furnished his house with furniture imported from England, including the finest Wilton carpets made to order to fit each room. The house, with most of its rich Georgian woodwork, survives today as one of the finest examples of late Georgian architecture in the upper Hudson valley. The single story wings were added in the 1840s. Later additions of a Victorian porch and trim were removed during a restoration in the 1950s.

Had it not been for the loyalist viewpoint he maintained during the early years of the Revolution, Peter Van Schaack (1747–1832) would likely have attained significance in the early years of the new republic. Instead, a seven-year exile in England (1778–85) forever hindered the attainment of such prominence and service to his country. Today scholars analyze his writings to better understand the loyalist point of view.

Though born of a moderately significant Dutch family at Kinderhook, he attained recognition through his ability rather than through his connections with important New York families. He attended Kings College (now Columbia University) in New York where he became friends with John Jay, Robert Livingston (Chancellor), Gouverneur Morris, and William Smith (lawyer, colonial New York historian, and Tory). A measure of his ability is the fact that he was assigned the responsible duty of revising the statutes of the Colony of New York in 1773. (In 1824–28 another distinguished Columbia County lawyer, Benjamin F. Butler, carried out this same task for the state.) After thirteen years in New York City he returned to Kinderhook in 1775, but not even Kinderhook was receptive to his views. When his exile began he had recently lost his first wife, Elizabeth Cruger, and was beginning to lose his eyesight.

His years in England proved profitable. Exposure to English culture and the great parliamentary system of government awakened in him a skepticism of English life. When he at last returned to America, he was greeted by John Jay, who had signed the paper for his expatriation.

He married a second time, Elizabeth Van Alen, a granddaughter of Luykas Van Alen (*p. 33*), and had nine children. He practiced law and undertook to providing formal training in law to more than a hundred young men. His "law school," which was maintained in his home, has been described by some historians as the first one in the country.

Henry Van Schaack (1733–1823), the eldest of the Van Schaack brothers, had the most colorful and varied career of the three. His name was much maligned by Albany County Dutch patriots prior to and during the Revolution. These men had good reason to distrust Henry Van Schaack: he had allied his interests with Englishmen as well as with Dutch; he had established a successful trading post at Detroit; he was the "neutral" stamp agent during

Henry Van Schaack, engraving. From Henry C. Van Schaack's Memoirs of the Life of Henry Van Schaack *(1892).*

the Stamp Act fracas in Albany; he was in league with Sir William Johnson; he was a wily politician; and above all, he effectively prevented the Van Rensselaers, Philip Schuyler, and others from claiming large, settled tracts of land in northeastern Columbia County. His assistance to New Englanders in the establishment of the Kings District (1772) was an affront to the powerful and patriotic Van Rensselaer family. It not only broke their claims to land but also caused them to lose some control over the local district militia. During the Revolution, Henry Van Schaack was exiled from New York and took up residence at Richmond, Massachusetts, just across the border. Here he lived until 1807, maintaining a lively interest in New York political growth, working in opposition to Shay's rebellion, and establishing the first carpet manufactory in Berkshire County. He was a trustee of Williams College. When he returned to his native Kinderhook, Henry Van Schaack built a house that still stands, overlooking the Hudson River at what is now Stuyvesant Landing.

William H. Ludlow House (1786), Route 23B, Claverack.

William Henry Ludlow (1740–1803) came in 1741 to Claverack, where his father had established a grain business. In 1771 he married Catherine Van Rensselaer, a sister of Philip Van Rensselaer of Albany and a cousin of the Claverack proprietors. William and Philip were good friends, and it would seem not coincidental that in 1786 they both built similar gambrel-roof Georgian style houses. Philip's house in Albany survives today as Historic Cherry Hill, a house museum. Similarly William Ludlow's house with many of its early furnishings remained almost entirely intact until recently.

The Ludlows were related by marriage to both Richard Morris and Robert Fulton. Associations with the latter gave the house and its contents much of its historical interest when it was opened some years ago as a "Fulton Museum" by a descendant, Robert Fulton Ludlow.

Although basically Georgian in style, the Ludlow house has features common to both earlier and later periods: the gambrel roof is a feature more popular in the 1760s, but a side door with its eliptical transom window is typical of Federal houses of a decade or two later. In most respects, however, it compares to the Van Schaack *(p. 53)*, Van Rensselaer *(p. 58)*, and Gilbert *(p. 92)* houses.

Hogeboom house, Broadstairs
(ca. 1750, major addition ca. 1800). Route 66, Ghent.

About 1740, Johannes Hogeboom, one of the earliest settlers in the northern part of Claverack (now the Town of Ghent), began a large farm and built a stone house. On the same site he opened an inn that forms the early rear wing of the large house called Broadstairs. The inn was a principal stopping place on the road from Albany to Boston. At this site Henry Knox stopped on a January night in 1776 while transporting cannon from Fort Ticonderoga to General Washington near Boston.

The main, or front, section of the house was built around 1800, probably by Johannes' son, Lawrence. It is a Federal structure retaining an elegant Palladian window. The front doorway and some interior details were remodeled around the 1830s in the Greek Revival style. The use of stone at this late period in Columbia County is unusual. The name "Broadstairs" is said to have derived from the stagecoach era, when a wide wood platform and stairway led up to the front door. The stairway was so wide, it is told, that one night an inebriated sheriff mistook it for the road and galloped up it.

57

Henry I. Van Rensselaer house, Hudson-Bush or Milburn (1785). Route 9H, Greenport.

Originally the lands at Claverack included present day Hudson, Greenport, Claverack, Hillsdale, and parts of Austerlitz and Ghent. The area had belonged to the Van Rensselaer family of Albany since the mid-seventeenth century. The lands were part of an early purchase made by an agent of the Van Rensselaer patroon in 1649. Though separate from Rensselaerwyck, they appear to have come under the jurisdiction of the manor established in 1685. However, in 1704 the fourth patroon and second lord of the manor, another Kiliaen Van Rensselaer (1663–1719) gave the Claverack lands to his younger brother Hendrik Van Rensselaer (1667–1740). Thereafter, the "Hendrik branch" of the family — and not the "manor branch" — were the proprietors of Claverack. Eventually some of the family began to move there. One such descendant of Hendrik's was his namesake and grandson, Henry I. Van Rensselaer (1742–1813), who was living in Claverack where he

was a captain of the foot company even before the Revolution. When war broke out he was an active patriot and served as colonel in the Continental Army. On June 6, 1785, he initiated the construction of his house. Lawrence Bushert and Johannes DeGroat were head masons and an Allen the head carpenter.

The following year he was appointed along with Peter Van Ness *(page 68),* a Judge of the County Court of Common Pleas, which convened in the new courthouse in Claverack *(see page 64).* By this time the city of Hudson, then comprising all of the Town of Greenport, had been established. Henry I. Van Rensselaer was elected a supervisor of the city in 1787–88 and named his farm and mansion "Hudson-Bush."

In its general form the Van Rensselaer house is similar to other Georgian mansions built in the upper Hudson valley in the last half of the eighteenth century. Comparable structures still standing are two of William

Johnson's houses in the Mohawk Valley, Philip Schuyler's house in Albany, and David Van Schaack's house in Kinderhook *(page 53).*

Smokehouse, Milburn (n. d.)

Behind the house is a rare survival — a brick smokehouse.

Whenever people undergo a communal rite of passage or a collective rebirth into a new world, an uncertain but exciting period of experimentation follows. Attempts are made to discover new ways of living in order to test the beliefs and values of the new society — in our case, the new nation. Lands in Albany County on the east side of the Hudson River below the southern boundary of Rensselaerwyck Manor became a separate and distinct county by state legislative action on April 4, 1786. The county was to be known as Columbia, named for the newest diety in the neoclassic pantheon. This goddess was the cohesive American embodiment of three Old World goddesses, Fame, Justice, and Wisdom. Americans invoked her spirit freely in the post-Revolutionary era.

In the new Columbia County, problems and opportunities in the government brought men of talent into public life, and ultimately one of these was to become President of his country. The freedom of opportunity that independence had created was in part responsible for two unusual and important planned settlements in Columbia County: the Quaker merchant settlement of Hudson and the Shaker Society settlement on Mt. Lebanon. Based on opposite premises, they were remarkably similar in their outward work, organization, and success. Population growth affected the nation's economic needs and capabilities, and scientific and technological innovation soon began to make themselves felt in the county. Scientific approaches to farming led to an improved husbandry. Wool growing became highly profitable and also provided a local source of raw materials for the important cloth manufacture that developed along the county's streams. The beginnings of our second revolution — the Industrial Revolution — developed early in the county as steam and waterpower were adapted for transportation and manufacture. In contrast, the descendants of early settlers continued their rural life in a less spectacular, but in the long run, more successful manner.

II
New American Experiments 1784–1830s

Robert R. Livingston

Robert R. Livingston (1746–1813), most extraordinary of all the Livingstons, had distinguished careers in government, the judiciary, diplomacy, agriculture, industry, and the arts. His spirited interests and efforts on behalf of the new nation were balanced between imaginative schemes and their practical application.

Chancellor Robert R. Livingston (1794), oil on canvas, 36" × 28¼", Gilbert Stuart. Courtesy Clermont State Historic Site, New York State Office of Parks and Recreation.

Robert Livingston's public career began at the age of thirty when he was a delegate to the Second Continental Congress. He subsequently assisted in the organization of the New York State government and was afterwards appointed chancellor, presiding over the State Chancery Court until 1801. In this capacity he administered the first oath of office to President George Washington in 1789.

Besides his roles in state and national government, he was actively interested in the economic and cultural development of the country. He was one of the founders and the first president of the New York Society for the Promotion of Agriculture, Arts, and Manufactures, begun in 1791. This Society was the parent organization of New York State's oldest museum, The Albany Institute of History and Art. A copy of Gilbert Stuart's portrait was made for that society by Ezra Ames.

Gilbert Stuart was a native Rhode Islander who had studied in England under Benjamin West. His facility for catching the spirit of his subject brought him influential and wealthy patrons in both New York and Philadelphia.

Chancellor Robert R. Livingston (1803), oil on canvas, 46¼" × 35¼", John Vanderlyn. Courtesy The New-York Historical Society. Gift of Mrs. Thomas Livingstone, 1876.

John Vanderlyn, a grandson of Pieter Vanderlyn who portrayed the Hudson valley Dutch during the 1730s, painted this portrait of Chancellor Livingston in Paris in 1803. The documents under Livingston's hand are inscribed "Plan for establishing an Academy of Fine Arts in New York," for which organization this portrait was made. The folded document near his elbow proclaims, "R.R. Livingston Minister Plenipoten from the United States of America. Paris." In that year he was the principal negotiator, arranging the Louisiana Purchase for the United States. During this time in France, he made preliminary studies for an experimental steamboat.

Clermont, Seat of the Chancellor Livingston, North River (1807), watercolor on paper, 4⅞" × 9½", P. Lodet. Courtesy Franklin D. Roosevelt Library, Hyde Park. Gift of Mark Eisener, 1933.

Clermont, the family estate *(see p. 48)* was bequeathed to Robert Livingston when his father died in 1775. The house, which stands today, remained the home of Robert's mother, Margaret Beekman Livingston *(see p. 47).* In 1783 Robert built a second Clermont several hundred yards south of his mother's house. Extensive English landscape gardens surrounded it.

At Clermont Robert was a scientific farmer, exchanging news and ideas with Thomas Jefferson among others. Livingston introduced into America in 1804 the fine-fleeced Merino sheep. The breeding of this Spanish sheep had a significant impact on cloth manufacture in the United States, for its fleece greatly improved the quality of American-made woolens.

This early view of the Chancellor's Clermont was one of nineteen illustrations done by P. Lodet. Most illustrations in his sketchbook are dated 1806 or 1807 and are of Hudson River valley scenes — apparently a record he made of his voyage from New York to the city of Hudson. He is believed to have been a Frenchman, but otherwise he is not identified.

Spafford's *Gazetteer* (1824) contains a description of the Chancellor's home:

The country-seat of the late Chancellor . . . deserves notice as one of the most extensively elegant in the State. It is situated on the E. bank of Hudson, in N. Latitude 42° 4' 39". Its front on the river is 104 feet, depth 91; and it consists of a main body of 2 stories and 4 pavilions. The south or garden-front is a green house, with bathing rooms and offices adjoining; over these is a large elegant breakfasting-room, and 4 bed-rooms. The second story is conveniently divided into 4 rooms, connected by a long gallery. One of the pavilions contains a well chosen library of about 4000 volumes, in various languages. The front faces a fine lawn, skirted on one side by a beautiful wood, on a bank raised about 10 feet, terminating in a second lawn, from the rear of which springs, precipitately, a rocky ridge, covered with shrubs, trees and evergreens, affording a fine rich background. This is balanced on the opposite side of the lawn by a beautiful avenue of locust trees, planted irregularly, through which winds the road to the House.

The house burned in 1909.

The Steamboat The North River *(ca. 1810), lithograph from drawing by C.B.J.F. de Saint-Memin (detail). Courtesy I. N. Phelps Stokes Collection, Prints Division, The New York Public Library, Astor, Lenox and Tilden Foundations. 8⁷/₁₆" × 12⅝"*

This is the earliest known representation of Robert Fulton's steamboat. Fulton and Robert Livingston had met in Paris in 1803, at which time they enthusiastically entered into plans and experiments for a steam propelled boat. They experimented with models on the Seine. In 1806 Fulton returned to America and began work in earnest. On August 13, 1807, the boat, first called the *North River Steamboat of Clermont* and later called the *Clermont* after the Chancellor's home, made its famous voyage to Albany — the first successful steamboat voyage in the world. Within a year's time, Hudson newspapers advertised not only steam travel to New York, but also lobster and ocean fish for the epicure dinner — delivered fresh on the new boat.

Like many Frenchmen, Saint-Memin (1770–1852) was a refugee of the French Revolution. He came to America in 1793 and remained until 1810, returning from France again in 1812 for about two years. While in the United States he painted some landscapes but made his livelihood by doing miniature portraits produced from the physionotrace, a device that made accurate profiles. He shows Fulton's steamboat on the lower Hudson River.

New Government and New Leaders

Columbia County was formed in 1786. At the new courthouse, county affairs were gradually put in order during the disruptive years that followed the Revolution. Around the turn of the nineteenth century a full generation of men born in the Revolutionary period began to enter public life. These ambitious and talented men made notable public servants. Some had the benefit of college training; most, however, were educated in their native villages and studied law as clerks to established lawyers. From their undistinguished origins some of these men went on to challenge, and ultimately to alter, the aristocratic premises of Federalism.

Columbia County was formed out of the extreme southeastern segment of Albany County in 1786. At that time Claverack, the most centrally located community, was designated the county seat. In December 1786, the newly formed Board of Supervisors recorded their purchase of land and appointed a committee of seven to supervise the construction of the court building. By November 1787, the building must have been completed for a traveler, John Enys, recorded at that time that he ". . . soon came to Claverack the Capital of Columbia County. Here [sic] are in this place several good handsome houses with a New Court House & Gaol . . . this place like the New City above Albany, Troy, has been entirely built since the peace . . ." The court building served as such until 1805 when the county seat was moved to Hudson. The Federal structure in Claverack was altered around 1830 with Greek Revival details at the portico and front entry.

A significant test of American law was tried at this courthouse in 1804. In 1803 *The Balance,* a Hudson newspaper, published a story containing a violent attack on President Jefferson's personal character. The Columbia County grand jury was convened to indict Harry Croswell, the editor, for libel. The State Attorney General Ambrose Spencer argued for the prosecution, while William W. Van Ness and Alexander Hamilton argued for the defense. In spite of a brilliant defense Croswell lost his case, but it was an important case that attracted national attention. Freedom of the press was in question. The issue debated revolved around whether or not the press has the right to expose the private affairs of public persons — a question still not fully resolved today.

*First Courthouse of Columbia County
(1787, remodeled ca. 1830). Route 23, Claverack*

Penfield map (detail, Columbia County Courthouse). Collection of the Columbia County Historical Society.

In 1799, the courthouse, surrounded by the houses John Enys wrote of, was on the principal road. The cupola centered on its roof is no longer there, leaving the courthouse looking very much the private residence that it has been since the late nineteenth century.

William W. Van Ness (1775–1823) was the son of William Van Ness and the nephew of Peter Van Ness. He, along with another county attorney, Elisha Williams, became well known in the first years of the nineteenth century. In the courtroom, Williams was characterized as "Hogarth, acting and describing, not drawing his pictures." His satiric and witty oratory contrasted to Van Ness' style: "smooth and mellifluous . . . with chaste and elegant simplicity, winning the hearts and judgments of the jury." The two men were close friends both personally and politically, but trials in which they opposed each other were regarded as rare entertainments. Van Ness and Williams, along with Jacob Rutsen Van Rensselaer became the Federalist leaders of the county. Van Ness himself was educated in his native village and studied law locally with John Bay (whose daughter he married) and briefly in New York. He was remembered for helping aspiring young men to enter the legal profession in a period when old-school lawyers maintained an aristocratic attitude toward the bar. In 1820 he was accused of accepting a bribe for securing the charter for the Bank of America. His innocence in the affair was established, but the episode may have affected his health, for he died shortly thereafter.

The date that the house was built is unknown. There is no question, however, that William W. built it, for it is so described in an 1843 deed. A tradition states that he "built the house for his daughter who married Henry Livingston." His oldest child, Analisa or Ann Eliza (b. 1791) married Livingston on December 28, 1816. However, Henry Livingston did not come into ownership of the property until December 1822, when William W. and his wife Jane sold it to him for eight thousand dollars. A series of deeds in 1822 between William W. and his sisters show that their father, William Van Ness (1736–1821), owned the property until

Talavera, the William W. Van Ness residence (ca. 1807–16). Route 9H, Claverack.

his death. He had purchased it in 1794 from the Van Rensselaer proprietors of Claverack. Although William W.'s father had owned it, William is described as in possession of it in these 1821 deeds. It is obvious that, though William W. had use of the property, he did not have the right to sell or give it to his daughter and son-in-law until he himself came to own it, which happened when his father died. If he did indeed build the house for his daughter, a building date of about 1816 is correct. It is possible, however, that he and his wife may have lived in the house. If that is true, a date soon after 1807, when he was appointed judge of the State Supreme Court, would be a likely time for him to have erected such a prestigious residence.

The architecture of the Van Ness house is an audacious break with earlier forms of Columbia County dwellings. Its most significant feature is its symmetry, achieved by balanced entrances in each wing rather than the usual central doorway and hall. The wings are original and each contains a curved paneled stairwell. The central portion of the house is divided into a formal parlor and a reception hall with a semicircular projection at the rear. Closets and other small, specialized rooms and the curved interior elements reflect innovations introduced into America by architects like Bulfinch, Latrobe, and L'Enfant. The great center pediment extending over the driveway is purely ornamental in character, since the protection from weather that it may afford does not extend to the two entrances. Many features of the house suggest the hand of an architect, but no plans or other evidence for this theory have been found.

Jacob Rutsen Van Rensselaer residence (ca. 1810). Route 23, Claverack.

Both the house and nearby mills *(p. 99)* were built by Jacob Rutsen Van Rensselaer. The traditional date of 1783 assigned to this house is unlikely since Van Rensselaer was only sixteen years old in that year, and the 1799 Penfeld map of Claverack indicates a less pretentious dwelling at the site. Jacob Van Rensselaer's public career began in 1809 when he was elected to the state assembly, in which he became a leader of the Federalists. Within the county political organization, he was part of an influential triumvirate along with Elisha Williams and William W. Van Ness. He served in the War of 1812 as general of the county militia. He later held other public offices including that of delegate to the 1821 state constitutional convention.

Architectural styles of the Federal Period offered choices of form not available before. Jacob Rutsen Van Rensselaer's house is less flamboyant than that of his colleague William W. Van Ness, but its canted corners enclose a pair of octagonal parlors. Such geometrical experimentations reflect the influence of the architect-designed houses of this period.

John P. Van Ness (ca. 1803), oil on canvas, ss 28" × 23", Gilbert Stuart. Private collection.

As a patriot and an early political and legal leader in the county, Peter Van Ness (1734–1804) established a precedent for his three sons. They all attended Columbia University and then studied in the offices of New York lawyers. Thereafter they held influential positions through the exceedingly varied presidental administrations of Jefferson, Madison, Monroe, Adams, Jackson, and Van Buren.

John P. Van Ness (1769–1846), the eldest son, began his career with a law practice in Claverack. In 1801 he was elected to Congress. The rest of his life was spent in Washington, D.C., where he was appointed by Presidents Jefferson and Madison as Brigadier-General and then Major-General of the Militia of the District of Columbia. He later served several terms as mayor of Washington and was a founder and first president of the Bank of the Metropolis of Washington. In the nation's capital, architect Benjamin Latrobe designed a residence for him in 1813. (The home was demolished in 1909.) His portrait by Gilbert Stuart probably dates from the early years in Washington, a brief period (1803–05) when Stuart was also there.

The second son, William P. Van Ness (ca. 1778–1826) is best known as Aaron Burr's second in the famous duel with Hamilton. His law practice and also Madison's appointment of him as judge of the United States District Court for the southern New York district gave him personal distinction.

Another Madison appointment placed Cornelius P. Van Ness (1782–1852), the third son, in the position of District Attorney for Vermont, where he later was elected governor. In Jackson's administration Cornelius Van Ness was appointed Ambassador to Spain.

James Vanderpoel (1787–1843) was born on a modest farm northeast of Kinderhook Village. Before the Revolution his father, Isaac, had been one of those prosperous Dutch farmers with extensive lands close to the Hudson River; because of his Tory activities during the Revolution, Isaac's property and personal estate were confiscated, although he was permitted to return to his native area. He then married Moyca Huyck and purchased a small farm in the Chatham Center region. Their second child and first son, James, was born in 1787. He was educated in Kinderhook Village and in 1804 began to study law under Francis Sylvester. About 1805 he went to Kingston and was an instructor at the Kingston Academy for two years. Later he resumed his legal training and had plans of going west after he acquired his license. However, in 1808, the same year he was admitted to the Columbia bar, he married Ann Doll, daughter of Domine George J. L. Doll, director of Kingston Academy.

Vanderpoel was closely associated with Martin Van Buren during the latter's years in Hudson and in 1812 succeeded Van Buren as County Surrogate. An important case in which Vanderpoel substituted for Van Buren against the sharp-witted Elisha Williams catapulted his legal career to success in 1814–15. For many years he was a member of the county's Federalist Party, in which he was associated with Jacob Rutsen Van Rensselaer and

James I. Vanderpoel (ca. 1821), oil on canvas,
31" × 24", Ammi Phillips.
Albany Institute of History and Art.

Ammi Phillips painted this portrait of Vanderpoel — and one of his wife Ann — in the early 1820s; the style seen here marks a distinct change from the pastel-hued portraits of county residents done by Phillips in 1814.

(continued from preceding page)
Elisha Williams. In 1828, however, he switched parties to follow Van Buren, thereby losing the race for Congress as a candidate of Jackson's supporters. Vanderpoel benefited from the patronage system introduced by Van Buren when Governor Throop, Van Buren's successor, appointed him circuit judge of the State Supreme Court in 1831. At this time he moved to Albany, where he was elected three times to the state assembly and where he remained until his death. (In 1841 one of his daughters, Elizabeth, married John Van Buren, a son of Martin and a promising young lawyer who attained prominence in the Democratic Party.)

About 1816 and in 1819 James and Ann Vanderpoel purchased adjacent lots in the village of Kinderhook and by 1820 had this substantial brick house built on them. The design of the building is attributed to Barnabas Waterman (1776–1839), a native of Bridgewater, Massachusetts, who came to Hudson early in his career. Waterman was a carpenter and builder, described in his obituary as a "master mechanic." As such, he served on several building committees for the city of Hudson and had a high reputation in his profession.

The house is one of the most sophisticated Federal Period houses in the Hudson River valley. Although a few similar brick houses exist in Columbia County (principally in the area in and around Hudson), none achieves the same pleasing balance of design and proportion. An unusual feature is the identical design of the front and back of the house.

Since 1924, the house has been owned by the Columbia County Historical Society. Known as the House of History, it is a restoration house museum of the Federal Period.

James Vanderpoel house (ca. 1816–20). Broad Street, Kinderhook.

Left. Hall and stairway, James Vanderpoel house.

The graceful and perfectly proportioned curves of the arch and stairway in the hall create a dramatic rhythm. Doorways are dressed with slender reeded columns and richly carved architraves. The remarkably successful whole appears to be the achievement of a designer-builder who combined his own talented ideas of design with elements borrowed from architectural copybooks.

Elliptical stairs and stairwells were introduced by Charles Bulfinch and popularized in Asher Benjamin's *American Builder's Companion* (1806). Ingenious framing, illustrated in Benjamin's work, supports the stairs, giving the illusion of no support at all.

Above. Parlor doorway (detail), James Vanderpoel house.

Delicate architectural ornament was a feature of Federal style. Such decorations were carved from wood with fine details moulded in plaster.

Martin Van Buren's rise to state and national political power was achieved when he and his contemporaries — like Jackson, Clay, and Calhoun — were successful in using manipulative politics to bring true democracy into government. Before Jackson's election (1828), national politics were dominated by the founding fathers and their political heirs. By 1830, however, the generally aristocratic political control of the Federal Period was replaced by politics in which the common citizen had greater representation. In this area Van Buren made important contributions to our modern political system.

In Kinderhook, where he was born, Martin Van Buren spoke two languages — Dutch and English. He grew up with an awareness of the social tensions between the Dutch and Anglo-Americans that had survived into the nineteenth century. During his youth and early manhood, county courts developed and changed, and political parties in the state split and regrouped and split again. Van Buren studied law with the respected Francis Sylvester in his native village. Then he spent a year in the New York City office of William P. Van Ness *(page 68)*. Van Buren returned to Kinderhook in 1803 and began his public career as a fence viewer. In 1808 he was appointed surrogate of the county and moved his practice to Hudson. Since William W. Van Ness had just been appointed to the Supreme Court, Van Buren became Elisha William's *(p. 67)* courtroom opponent in many cases. Van Buren remained active in county affairs until 1815 when he was appointed state attorney general and moved to Albany. He became governor

Martin Van Buren (1828), oil on canvas, 52¾" × 41", Ezra Ames.
Collection Albany Institute of History and Art, on permanent loan from the City of Albany.

in 1828 and resigned in 1829 in order to accept President Jackson's appointment as secretary of state.

Ezra Ames' portrait of Van Buren is one of a series of seven governors of New York that Ames painted, all now on permanent loan to the Albany Institute of History and Art from the City of Albany. Ames, a native of Massachusetts, began his Albany painting career as a sign painter in 1793. In his own lifetime he established an influential reputation among contemporaries. His use of classical architecture, law books, and documents for formal commissioned portraiture echoes Vanderlyn's and Stuart's efforts of twenty-five years before. Before and after Ames, this iconography was frequently used by provincial painters in New England and New York.

Martin Van Buren's gravestone.
Kinderhook cemetery, Albany Avenue, Kinderhook.

Van Buren was buried in 1862 in the Van Buren family plot along with other members of his family in the cemetery of his native village.

New Ideas for the New Society

There were other areas of new endeavor besides government and the law. An important field in which new ideas were tested was education. In 1804, Jesse Torrey established a free public library at New Lebanon. The theories he put in practice there became the pattern for free public libraries as we know them today. Another educator, Andrew M. Carshore, established two of Columbia County's important early schools where he supervised the education of many who went on to serve in influential public careers. In those days academy education often included ornamental arts such as drawing, music, and design. Carshore was accomplished in these fine arts, as well as in the traditional school curriculum.

In 1800 public libraries were not new. One, for example, had been established in Hudson in 1786. Jesse Torrey (1787–n.d.), who was born and grew up in New Lebanon, believed that libraries should be not only public but also free. In *The Intellectual Torch* he described "the juvenile society for the acquisition of knowledge," which he had established in New Lebanon in 1804. He had assembled a collection of books and made them available for borrowing to the young people of the community. Initially he had limited his project to young people, but he later came to realize that people of all ages, sexes, and classes would profit from free public libraries, for without books literacy would be a wasted art. Over the years he developed his idea.

Although he was born and grew up in New Lebanon, he spent most of his life in Philadelphia where, in 1817, he published his influential work *The Intellectual Torch*. Through this book and personal contacts with presidents, congressmen, statesmen, and public officials — particularly in Pennsylvania, Maryland, and Virginia — he developed his idea that schools were not enough and that his plan for the efficient and economical "universal dissemination of knowledge by means of free public libraries" was worthwhile. To implement the

Jesse Torrey (1817), engraving, inscribed "Ra. Peale, Del., Goodman & Piggott, Sc." From Portraiture of Slavery *and* The Intellectual Torch *(1817).*

Jesse Torrey silhouette (n.d.).

plan, he recommended that local and national governments should be the instruments for legally establishing and financially aiding such libraries and that a competent local committee should choose suitable books. As the result of his efforts, he is today regarded as the founder of the free circulating library system.

Robert Piggott and Charles Goodman had served their apprenticeships as engravers with David Edwin of Philadelphia. In that city from 1816 until about 1822 they had a partnership and did considerable work for annuals and periodicals. Besides Torrey's portrait, they also engraved the illustrations designed by Torrey depicting the conditions of American slaves, which appeared in Torrey's *Portraiture of Slavery* (1817). The drawing for Torrey's portrait is believed to be by Raphaelle Peale, son of Charles Willson Peale and himself an artist whose major works were portraits and still lifes but who supported himself by painting miniatures and executing cutout silhouettes.

The silhouette is reproduced from a later commemorative edition of the *Intellectual Torch*. Its maker is not known.

In March 1792 the commissioners of the federal buildings sponsored a competition for designs for the Capitol and the home for the president. Dr. William Thornton and John Hoban, both trained architects, submitted the winning entries. However, the competition inspired national interest, and en-

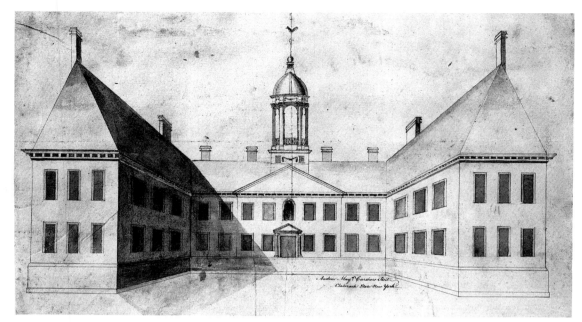

"Respective [sic] View of the Federal House," Capitol Competition drawing (1792), pen and ink on paper, Andrew Mayfield Carshore. Courtesy the Maryland Historical Society.

tries from a variety of people were submitted. One of these came from Andrew Mayfield Carshore, who lived in Columbia County from 1777 until about 1810. Besides submitting plans for the Capitol, and for the president's house he also drew a design for a presidential canopy.

This young Irishman, while strolling on Dublin docks, was pressed into the service of the British army in which he served under General Burgoyne at Saratoga. It is not known whether Carshore escaped or was released but he may have arrived in Kinderhook with captive Burgoyne's entourage en route to Boston on the night October 22 *(see p. 53)*. He taught at Kinderhook, but in 1780 went to Claverack, where he assumed the duties of principal of Washington Seminary, founded in 1777 by Domine Gebhard *(see pp. 43 and 106)*. Here, for twenty-five years, Carshore worked to establish education in the classical tradition and supervised the training of such men as John and Cornelius Van Ness and Jacob Rutsen Van Rensselaer *(see pp. 68 and 67)*. The high reputation of the Washington Seminary was due to Carshore's achievements as its principal. In 1805 he accepted an appointment as principal of the Hudson Academy, which had been founded by the city's leading citizens, and for five years worked there to establish Hudson's first successful academy. The school was located on Prospect Hill *(see pp. 98 and 120)*, where the incorporators erected a substantial three-story brick building. The date of Carshore's move to Hudson coincides with the move of the county seat there. Connections with prominent lawyers apparently drew him to activity in county government in which he served as clerk to the County Board of Supervisors in 1798–99, 1801–05, and 1809. As Carshore was especially renowned for his fine penmanship, the supervisors' minutes for those years must have been elegant documents, although they perished in the courthouse fire of 1908. (Examples of his calligraphy were exhibited in 1867 at the celebration of the Claverack Church centennial.)

Carshore's "Respective View" was submitted along with elevations, floor plans, and a perspective drawing that has been identified by Jeanne Butler as the first known in the history of American design and is one of eleven surviving plans for the Capitol. The proposal is based on English Georgian styles, and its cupola is reminiscent of those used in late seventeenth- and early eighteenth-century English Renaissance/baroque buildings. His design shows a conservatism of style reflective of building habits in the upper Hudson valley region. While Carshore's name is not associated with the design of any Columbia County buildings, it seems likely that this plan was not his only effort.

Quaker Merchants at Hudson

In 1783, Thomas Jenkins, acting on behalf of an association of thirty New England proprietors, purchased large tracts of land from members of the Hardick family, from Peter Hogeboom, Jr., and from the widow of Johannes Van Alen. The new settlers at Claverack Landing came principally from Providence and Newport, Rhode Island, and Nantucket and Edgartown, Massachusetts. In 1784, the New Englanders formulated plans for laying out a city in a grid pattern at Claverack Landing. In April 1785 the city of Hudson was incorporated. Just a year later the *New York Journal* reported that Hudson had several fine wharves, four large warehouses, a sperm oil works, 150 dwellings, shops, barns, a distillery, and 1500 people. Tanning, sail making, rope making, and shipbuilding were important industries. Shops and taverns increased in number.

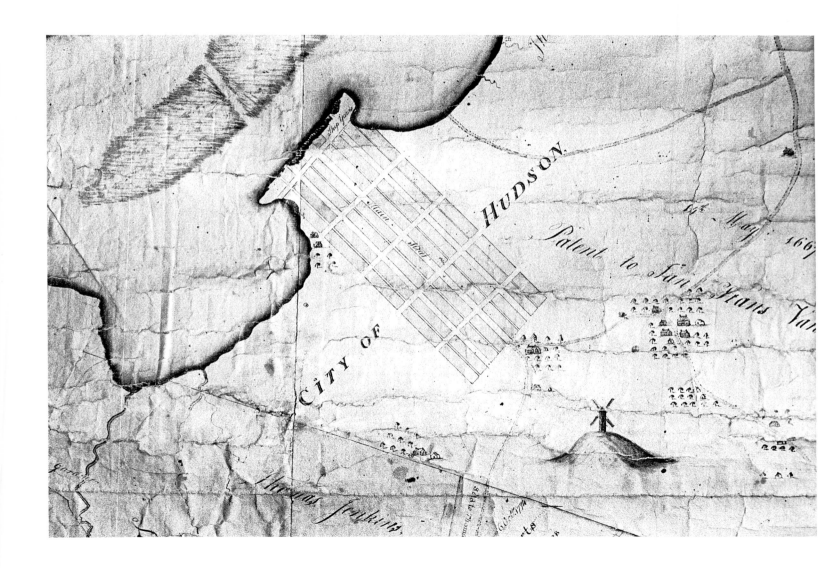

Hudson City (ca. 1806), water color,
P. Lodet, 3¾″ × 10⅜″.
Courtesy Franklin D. Roosevelt Library, Hyde Park.
Gift of Mark Eisener to Franklin D. Roosevelt, 1933.

Lodet's painting, the earliest known view of Hudson, indicates the well-developed city with warehouses and wharves at its shore line. Lodet made a journey up the Hudson River valley in 1806 and 1807, during which time he made watercolor sketches in a book. This view of Hudson was the northern-most point which he illustrated.

Penfield map (detail, The City of Hudson).
Collection Columbia County Historical Society.

The city is the only municipality in the county that did not originate at some creek or highway crossing or at a mill site on a stream. Instead a rise of land that jutted out between two bays into the Hudson River was the site selected for a city whose shipping and commercial activities created instant and unparalleled growth.

Hudson has retained the plan illustrated in 1799, although the city has expanded beyond the size indicated here. The principal difference today is that South Bay has been filled in.

75

Robert Jenkins house (1811). 113 Warren Street, Hudson.

role in the first decades of Hudson's history. In that period far-sighted city planning was begun; and immediate attention was given to the need for urban water supply, transportation, and education in the new city.

Architecturally the Jenkins house is a fully developed example of the type of Federal style house found frequently in the Hudson valley. It compares with the Vanderpoel house in Kinderhook in its proportions and in the arrangement of features on the front facade.

The house was given by Robert Jenkins' granddaughter to the Hendrick Hudson Chapter of the DAR and is today a museum of Hudson and Greenport history. In the remodeling of the house early in the twentieth century for use by the DAR, virtually the entire interior was changed. The exterior, however, preserves the sophisticated appearance that characterized the architecture of the city's early years.

Robert Jenkins was active in Hudson city politics, following after his uncle Thomas Jenkins who had been the leading figure in the founding of Hudson. Robert was twice mayor (1808–12 and 1815–19) and one of the anti-Federalist leaders in the city. He frequently met with other members at party headquarters in the lower rooms of the Hudson *Bee,* a partisan newspaper brought to Hudson with its editor, Charles Holt, by the anti-Federalists in 1802. Hudson businessmen tended to be an anti-Federalist faction frequently in opposition to the agricultural and domestic industries in the rest of the county. The Jenkins family played a leading

In 1820 William Guy Wall published his *Hudson River Portfolio,* which included twenty engraved views of Hudson River scenes. He was a native of Dublin and arrived in New York in 1818. His watercolor paintings, which were preliminary to the *Portfolio* engravings, won wide popularity.

The watercolors included this house of Samuel Plumb situated on a plateau above South Bay and the Hudson River, with Mt. Merino and the Catskills in the background. Samuel Plumb was a New Englander who followed the original proprietors to Hudson. Thomas Jenkins had purchased numerous tracts of land around Hudson, and in 1811 his heirs sold one of these tracts to Samuel Plumb, who built this house. Especially interesting in Wall's record of the house are the symmetrically arranged dependencies at either side of the house, examples of Federal Period design and landscape that no longer exist.

The design of the house is another example of experimentation in the Federal Period. The two-story structure has semi-octagonal extensions at each end of the first floor and a small central third-story block in the middle of the roof. The Federal decorative features of the house are exceptional and include a long veranda, semi-elliptical fanlights, keystones, and decorative scrolls.

After the Plumb family sold the property in 1835 or 36, it was briefly held by other owners and then purchased in 1838 by Dr. Oliver Bronson of Hudson. The research of Jane B. Davies has documented that in 1839 Bronson employed Alexander Jackson Davis, a leading architect of the time, for "refitting" the house and designing stables, trellises, and "various fixtures and embellishments." This included the extension of the eaves and the addition of ornamental brackets. The house and the stable south of the house are the ear-

View near Hudson, New York, looking Southwest toward Mt. Merino (ca. 1819), watercolor on paper, 14" × 21", William Guy Wall.
Courtesy The New-York Historical Society, New York City.

liest existing examples of Hudson River "bracketed" style known to have been designed by Davis. Ten years later Davis was again commissioned to make alterations — this time in the Italianate style.

With these alterations, the Bronson house is an early example of innovative work by Davis to adapt an earlier house to "a more rural aspect in accord with romantic theories of country-house design which were then just beginning to emerge in America. These theories emphasize the importance of architectural irregularities and picturesque details in achieving a harmony of buildings with their natural landscape settings."

77

Capt. John Hathaway house (1790s).
Formerly 140 Warren Street, Hudson.

Elliptical stairway, Samuel Plumb house,
Route 9, Hudson.

This stairway, which rises to the third floor, is an exceptional example of a characteristic design of the Federal Period *(see p. 19).*

According to records in the family Bible, owned by the Hendrik Hudson Chapter of the DAR, John Hathaway came to Hudson in 1784 and engaged in the freight and passenger business on the Hudson River and also traded at Mediterranean ports. In the 1790's he advertised that his passenger accommodations were the finest available on the river. Active in various civic affairs, he is also associated with a number of charitable works including the direction of the city's early poor house (1801). He lived in this house at 140 Warren Street until his death in 1818; it descended to members of his family who occupied it until 1906; it was later converted to a garage and subsequently demolished in the 1930s.

In all likelihood, the John Hathaway house is the one structure in Hudson that best expressed the prosperity of the city's founders. An elegant example of Federal style, it included nearly all the decorative conceits available in that period: fluted pilasters, Ionic capitals, a carved sunburst friese, and a gallery topped with urns. Other houses in Hudson, in Kinderhook, and near Chatham *(p. 94)* share some of these elements, but none combines all of them in a tour de force like Hathaway's house. In its formal Federal style it compares with houses built on the coast of Hathaway's native Massachusetts, especially with existing houses in Salem. Related examples of Federal architecture appear across the Hudson River in Athens and (formerly) in Albany.

The interior was described as in keeping with the exterior. Judging by fireplace mantels from this house (now preserved in the Elks lodge in Hudson), the interior must have been elegant indeed.

Alexander Jenkins house (by 1799; renovations ca. 1818 and ca. 1830s). Joslyn Boulevard, Greenport.

Alexander Jenkins is reported to have been one of the crew of Capt. Solomon Bunker's ship the *American Hero,* which in 1797 brought from the Pacific the largest cargo of sperm oil brought to the United States up to that time. Alexander Jenkins is believed to have been one of the numerous members of the Jenkins family who came from Providence and Nantucket to Hudson in the years following the founding of the city. He was called Capt. Alexander Jenkins and was likely to have been involved in Hudson's shipping enterprises. A number of recorded land transactions in which he took part suggest that he had an interest in Hudson real estate as well.

The most interesting aspect of the house is its remarkable combination of Dutch and New England features, to which were later added Federal style details and Greek Revival renovations. The central bay of the house is two rooms deep on each floor with a generous hallway running the depth of the house on both levels. The wings are one room deep and there is no hallway access to the left wing. This plan has provincial echoes of the sophisticated form of houses like those of Joab Center and William W. Van Ness *(pp. 83, 66).* The columned front porch and the grille work covering the eyebrow windows are Greek Revival features probably introduced by Capt. Alexander Robinson of Brooklyn, who purchased the house in 1828. At that time the front slope of the roof was raised to accommodate three rooms across the front of the attic.

Bank of Hudson (ca. 1809). 116 Warren Street, Hudson.

In the once- and later-prosperous city of Hudson, which was just then going through the depression brought on by the 1807 embargo on international trade, 1809 was not a year to be organizing a bank. While the embargo forced American manufacturers to develop, it hurt farmers and shipping merchants, the mainstay of Hudson's economy. John C. Hogeboom, however, was determined to make a go at it. The Bank of Hudson was chartered in 1809, and Hogeboom built for his bank this elegantly restrained urban structure. During the following years, including the War of 1812, Hudson's economy faltered, but the building survived as the Hogeboom residence.

When the former bank became Hogeboom's residence (ca. 1820), the original entrance, centered in the facade, was moved to its present side location, and a Greek Revival portico was added, Judging by changes in brickwork, the original entrance had a fan-shaped transom window complemented by the two flanking medallions. Marble medallions, flanking marble pilasters, and an ornamental frieze form a striking composition combining Federal motifs with some of the earliest use of Greek Revival features. The architectural quality of the house is in keeping with several other surviving Federal Period houses built in and around Hudson at the turn of the nineteenth century.

From the time of its settlement in 1784, the New Englanders had endeavored to work with members of the Dutch community that had preceded them and included the Dutch on the Common Council and other civic capacities. John C. Hogeboom was from Ghent and is the only documented Dutch descendant to have been so significantly involved in Hudson business affairs and to have built so imposing a structure amidst the New Englanders.

Capitol and frieze (detail), Bank of Hudson

Decorations similar to these appear on John Hathaway's house, and the sunbursts in the frieze recur in Federal buildings around the county. The origin of such embellishment is not known, but it is likely that such decorative elements were ordered from a common source.

Joab Center house (ca. 1812–21). Route 9, Greenport.

Traditionally Joab Center is said to have been a ship captain, who, after his retirement had this house built to resemble a ship. If a ship captain, he was also one of the Hudson merchants who turned in the 1800s to fine-wool speculation *(see p. 96)*. He purchased a farm in Claverack (1813) and another in Hillsdale (1814). Between 1812 and 1825 he purchased ten adjacent parcels of land in the vicinity of the Farmers' Turnpike, near present-day Joslyn Boulevard and Fairview Avenue, where the house is located. This farm was one of several around Hudson that specialized in wool growing. Center was in business with other Hudson merchants who advertised sheep for sale. At this site, sometime after 1812, he built the "turtle house," a local name based on the roof line's resemblance to a turtle's back.

While the appearance of the house may be reminiscent of a sailing vessel or a turtle, it is also a distinguished example of the innovative forms used in Federal Period architecture. Like Talavera, the central part of the house is flanked by smaller wings that contain the entrances. The central oval configuration is divided into a pair of large matching parlors, so that front and rear facades and main floor plan are symmetrical. Its decorative details are similar to the Vanderpoel house in Kinderhook *(p. 69)* and to the Hathaway and Hogeboom houses in Hudson *(pp. 79, 81)*.

Marble medallion, Bank of Hudson

The simple, low-relief drapery recalls the Adam brothers' interpretation of classical motifs.

The Hudson Almshouse/Lunatic Asylum (1818). From a woodcut published in the Rural Repository, *1814. State Street at Fourth Street, Hudson.*

Under the New York laws of 1778 towns and cities were responsible for the care of their poor. In Hudson the first house for such care was purchased in 1801 and served until 1818, when the present large stone structure was built for the purpose by Ephraim Baldwin under the supervision of Judah Paddock, John Tallman, and Barnabas Waterman of the building committee. The plan of the structure is based on one drawn by Robert Jenkins *(p. 76);* its construction cost $5100.

In 1830 the city abandoned the building; and that same year Dr. Samuel White, who had practiced medicine in Hudson since about 1795, established an insane asylum in the building. White, assisted by his son Dr. George H. White, specialized in humane care of mental patients and had considerable success in curing some of them. Dr. Samuel White was also an important surgeon in New York State, one of the founders of the Columbia County Medical Association (1806) and in 1843 president of the State Medical Society.

When the state asylum at Utica was opened, Dr. White's asylum was closed. In 1851 the Hudson Female Academy was established in the building under the direction of Reverend J. B. Hague. Among the faculty was Henry Ary *(see p. 126)* who taught painting and drawing to fourth-year students. After 1865, when the Academy moved to another location, the building served as a residence. Today it is the Hudson Area Library.

This imposing stone building is related in style to the house of Robert Jenkins, who is said to have drawn the plans for the almshouse. It is a unique local example of surviving Federal architecture intended for institutional use.

HUDSON LUNATIC ASYLUM.

At Mount Lebanon more than thirty buildings remain of the former lead community of the United Society of Believers in Christ's Second Appearing, commonly called Shakers; its last members left the region in 1947. This Registered National Historic Landmark site is now occupied by the Darrow School, the Sufi religious order, and several private owners. Nine members of a small English sect, the first Shakers, arrived in America in 1774. A decade later, shortly before fellow American converts (who were to number perhaps twenty thousand in all) took control of the movement, New Hampshire convert Moses Johnson directed construction of the Shaker church here. Names of the other carpenter-builders of one hundred or more austere dormitory dwellings, industrial shops, laboratories, and farm buildings originally composing this monastic village are mostly unknown.

In the autumn of 1819, Benjamin Silliman, a traveler from Hartford, Connecticut, visited the Mount Lebanon Shaker village. In 1820 and 1824, he published editions of his travels and included a description of the physical appearance and social order of the Shaker community. The Yale professor made astute observations about their way of life:

The property is all in common. The avails of the general industry are poured into the treasury of the whole; individual wants are supplied from a common magazine, or store house, which is kept for each family, and ultimately, the elders invest the gains in land and buildings, or sometimes in money, or other personal property, which is held for the good of the society.

. . . [E]ven their stone walls are constructed with great regularity, and of materials so massy, and so well arranged, that unless overthrown by force, they may stand for centuries . . .

Besides agriculture, it is well known, that the Shakers occupy themselves much, with mechanical employments. The productions of their industry and skill, sieves, brushes, boxes, pails and other domestic utensils are every where exposed for sale, and are distinguished by excellence of workmanship. Their garden seeds are celebrated for goodness and find a ready market. They have many gardens, but there is a principal one of several acres which I am told exhibits superior cultivation.

Their females are employed in domestic manufactures and house work, and the community is fed and clothed principally by its own production. . . .

Their house of public worship is painted white, and is a neat building, whose appearance, would not be disreputable to any sect. . . .

Their buildings are closely arranged, along a street of a mile in length. All of them are comfortable, and a considerable proportion are large. They are, almost without exception, painted of an ochre yellow, and, although plain, they make a handsome appearance. The utmost neatness is conspicuous in their fields, gardens, courtyards, out houses, and in the very road; not a weed, not a spot of filth, or any nuisance is suffered to exist.

. . . and every thing bears the impress of labour, vigilance and skill, with such a share of taste, as is consistent with the austerities of their sect.

Shaker stone barn of the North Family (1859).
Mount Lebanon.

Originally built with a flat roof, this structure was completed in 1858 under the supervision of its designer, elder George Wickersham. It was one of the largest stone barns in America (192 feet long, and 50 feet wide, with four floors) before it burned in September 1972. The functional design of the barn is typical of Shaker ingenuity: because it is built into a hillside, it can be entered on the ground level or on any of its three other levels; hayracks entered on the fourth floor, and hay was dropped into a haymow on the third floor (or into two interior silos), then fed down to the cattle stanchioned on the second floor. Manure was carried from the second floor in buckets on an overhead rail to one end of the floor and then dropped into wagons on the first floor to be carted outside.

Shaker Second Family stone dam and mill site (ca. mid-nineteenth century). Mount Lebanon.

In a ravine to the west of the community of the Shaker Second Family at Mount Lebanon are two rock dams, now mostly unknown or forgotten. On these sites the Shakers built two of their many mills. How these massive stones might have been moved to the site is unknown although Shaker ingenuity and inventiveness are well known. The stones were laid — apparently without mortar — and are so carefully placed that the dam was watertight; it still resists the effects of spring floods and winter snow and ice.

The Church Family second meeting house (1822 –24). Mount Lebanon.

This building housed the parent ministry for all Shakers; and, therefore, the cost and labor of construction in 1824 was shared by several Shaker communities. Its unusual barrel or rainbow roof spans a meeting room sixty-three feet wide and seventy-eight feet long. The wing on the south side housed members of the ministry, elders, and eldresses. It was painted white to conform to Shaker Millennial Law (Section 1, Articles 3 and 6) that states "the meeting house should be painted white without and a bluish shade within. . . . No buildings may be white save the meeting houses." Millennial Law forbade beauty for its own sake. On the other hand, by designing to strictly functional requirements, the Shakers achieved a quality of proportion in line and mass that resulted in buildings of enduring beauty.

Today the former meeting house is the library of Darrow School, which has been sensitive in the use and preservation of it and other structures of the former Church and North Families.

Federal Descendants of the Dutch Settlers

In the Federal Period, the descendants of Dutch and German settlers retained significant remnants of their distinctive cultures. Both Dutch and German were used until the middle of the nineteenth century (and in isolated instances, much later than that). Church life in New York, which differed from the New England town meeting tradition (where temples, not taverns, were the political arenas), was important to the continuity of rural community life. In spite of these apparent ethnic differences, descendants of the earliest settlers also achieved a place within Federal society.

John and Catherine Vanderpoel Pruyn (ca. 1810),
silhouette, 5⅝" × 8⅝", maker unknown.
Private collection.

Arent Pruyn came from Albany to Kinderhook in the early eighteenth century. One of his sons, John Pruyn (1748–1815), inherited and maintained the extensive family farm and married Catherine Vanderpoel (1746–1826). Their nine children grew up during the Revolution and in the early years of the Federal Period. Five of their nine children married Van Vleck offspring *(see p. 89)*. Some of their sons and grandsons were among the most eminent local physicians and lawyers of the nineteenth century. Their daughters and graddaughters often married professional people. Members of this large family lived near the homestead and farm, which remained in the family for one more generation. A full collection of family portraits owned by descendants survive today.

Silhouettes, a fashionable and quick form of portraiture in the Federal Period, are said to have originated with Etienne de Silhouette (1709–67), a French author and minister of finance who was ridiculed for his petty economies. The name *silhouette* was applied to characterize the economy of the sketchy portraits. Another source indicates that Silhouette himself made such portraits and lent his name to the form. The style came to America from France around the last quarter of the eighteenth century and was popular until the 1850s.

The silhouettes of John and Catherine Pruyn are in their original frame and glass, which is ornamented with eglomise decoration. John Pruyn's hair is drawn in ink on the paper rather than having been cut out.

Abraham I. Van Vleck (1740–1824) came with his brother from New Jersey to Kinderhook in the 1760s. After the Revolution, his brother Isaac moved to Onondaga where he was one of the earliest settlers and among the first to establish salt production there. Abraham and his wife Jannetje (1744–1825) remained at Kinderhook and raised ten children, five of whom married children of John and Catherine Pruyn *(see p. 88)*. Abraham Van Vleck and three of his sons were probably engaged in farming, as well as in establishing a large general store at Kinderhook. The Van Vleck family became prominent landowners and Kinderhook merchants during the Federal Period, and in subsequent generations spread throughout the county.

Abraham and Janetje Vosburgh Van Vleck (ca. 1800), water color, oval ss 3¾" × 2¾", painter unknown. Private collection.

Water color portraits like these of the Van Vlecks are an elaboration on the silhouette. Although line details and wash or colors were added, they did not require long sittings and were inexpensively produced by traveling artists who took up temporary residence in a community. Artists like these brought their skills to rural areas outside urban art centers. One such was D. H. Cromwell who advertised his work in 1808.

mate, essential part of family life. By the 1820s a printed form was adopted for preparing inventories of the personal estates of the desceased. This form specified that family portraits were not to be listed as part of the assets of an estate but as essential household articles reserved for the widow or minor children. This stipulation may also account, at least in part, for the great proportion of surviving portraits compared to paintings of other types.

Peter Van Vleck (1771–1831) was Abraham Van Vleck's first son. In 1792 he married Catherine Pruyn (1746–1826) and had nine children. Peter Van Vleck is said to have owned seven farms between Kinderhook and the town of Canaan. Around 1825 he built a substantial brick house, which serves today as the National Union Bank of Kinderhook. The inventory of his estate (on file in the Columbia County Surrogate's office), reveals not only a full, well-furnished household but also his interest in farming and farms, the contents of a fully stocked store supplying textiles and other household merchandise, and ownership of a cider brandy distillery.

Peter Van Vleck's inventory also reveals that the law had come to recognize portraiture as an inti-

Peter Van Vleck (ca. 1800), water color, oval 5½" × 3¾", painter unknown. Private collection.

Sarah Pruyn (Mrs. Arent) Van Vleck (ca. 1810),
water color, ss 4⅜″ × 3⅜″,
painter unknown. Private collection.

The "Vedder Church" (Dutch Reformed Church) (1824).
Gallatinville.

Traditionally the church was the ornament of a Dutch community. This cultural trait carried into the American nineteenth century, as churches continued to be the center of community life. The first structure used by this congregation was built in 1748 and followed the simple, square, hipped-roof form of many other Dutch churches in the Hudson valley. That building was abandoned in 1822, and the next church was similar in style to churches built by New Englanders in Hudson and in the northeastern part of the county. The church has had many names: Stissick, Livingston Manor, Ancram, Mt. Ross, Greenbush, and Gallatin. It is best known, however, as "The Vedder Church" in honor of the Reverend Herman Vedder *(p. 91).*

Sarah Pruyn Van Vleck (1782–1869), one of the five children of John and Catherine Pruyn *(see p. 88),* married Arent Van Vleck, a son of Abraham and Jannetje Van Vleck. Arent Van Vleck was involved with his brothers, Peter and Henry, in business and land affairs in Kinderhook.

The difference in costume between Sarah Van Vleck and her mother-in-law Jannetje Van Vleck *(see p. 89)* reflects not a difference in painting dates but a difference in generation. Older persons tended to wear the styles of their prime years: thus Jannetje's shawl and cap and Abraham's peruke and low collar are in contrast to the current Federal Period styles in the portraits of short-haired Peter Van Vleck and Empire-gowned Sarah Pruyn Van Vleck. Another portrait of Sarah Van Vleck was painted late in life by James E. Johnson, a portrait painter who lived in Kinderhook for twelve years *(see p. 129).*

Organ, The Vedder Church (ca. 1872).

This remarkable organ is of unusual quality for a rural church. Besides its fine tone, its design is richly ornamental.

The Reverend Herman Vedder (ca. 1860s), 18" × 14½", artist unknown. Courtesy The Vedder Church (The Reformed Dutch Church of Gallatin). Gift of George Esselstyn and Edward Van Alstyne.

Herman Vedder (1777–1873) graduated from Union College at Schenectady in 1799 and in 1803 began his term as pastor at what was then the "Greenbush Church." He retired in 1863 but frequently took part in services until his death. His long tenure at the church resulted in a continuity of rural community life through changing decades of the nineteenth century.

The portrait of Reverend Vedder is a type that appears with frequency in the county during the 1860s and 1870s. More than one artist appears to have worked in a style that closely imitates the realism of photography.

Federal Descendants of New England Settlers

During the Revolutionary years, the northeastern quarter of what was to become Columbia County was called Kings District. After creation of Columbia County in 1786, this district was divided into five townships, with its citizens, mostly of New England origin, already outstanding practitioners of the town meeting form of government. Farming, milling, domestic cloth manufacture, and trading were the basis for the economy of these towns, which, within three decades after the Revolution, reached the considerable prosperity reflected today in some of the fine houses built in that period.

Elisha Gilbert house (1795). Route 20, New Lebanon.

Elisha Gilbert II was born ca. 1750, a native of New Lebanon. Family records indicate that he was a captain in the regiment of William B. Whiting (of Canaan) at the Battle of Saratoga in 1777. Later, in 1791, he was commissioned a major of the local militia. Upon returning to New Lebanon after the war, he is said to have operated the mill begun by his father (traditional date, 1751), farmed, and apparently engaged in financial and real estate dealings. Land in this vicinity was not properly titled until 1793 when the state legislature vested ownership in persons in possession of the land. The Gilbert house and site of the mill appear to be located in what was John I. Van Rensselaer's (and others') Mawighanunk patent (1743), described as 4380 acres on the Wyomanock Creek, which runs through the heart of the Lebanon valley eventually emptying into the Kinderhook Creek. A traditional date for the house is 1794, although other sources state the house was begun in 1794 and finished in 1795. When he built his home, Gilbert agreed with his Masonic Unity Lodge No. 9, formed in 1789, to provide a meeting room on the garret floor.

The house is similar to several other large gambrel-roof mansions (e.g., Ludlow house, *p. 56*), with decorative details reflective of English Georgian taste and the beginnings of Federal style.

Masonic symbol (ca. 1805), Elisha Gilbert house, oil on plaster, maker unknown. Route 20, New Lebanon.

The most extraordinary part of Elisha Gilbert's house is the masonic meeting room in the garret. The entire third floor is a single open room with a vaulted ceiling. It was decorated in the early nineteenth century with murals depicting masonic symbols. Two chimneys in the room are also decorated. The ceiling, too, was once covered with masonic symbols, but these were in poor repair and were painted over when the wall murals were restored in 1890 by the then owner of the house.

Elisha's son Elisha Gilbert III (1796–1852) inherited the house, and the room was used by the Unity Lodge until 1850, when a dispute between Elisha and the lodge resulted in its meeting elsewhere. The Unity Lodge is one of New York State's oldest masonic lodges, and the Gilbert house is its oldest existing meeting place.

Reuben Moore house (1830), water color on paper, 14¾" × 21¾", (detail). Charlotte Temple Moore. Chatham. Courtesy The New-York Historical Society.

Ruben Moore (1768–1858) was the fourth child of Noadiah and Anna Moore who had settled at Spencertown by 1770. By 1796 Reuben had married Levina Dean (ca. 1773–1834), raised six children, operated the prosperous farm pictured. Reuben Moore's grandson wrote of him,

he was a well educated man and called a philosopher. He was a good business man and owned a large farm in Chatham. He was of good judgment and moral character and highly respected by all. He was Master of Chancery (1813), and Coroner . . . (1799) and . . . (1801), in Columbia County. He was of medium height, would weigh about 160; had blue eyes and brown hair.

A fine portrait, now unlocated, was made of Reuben Moore around 1810.

This watercolor of Reuben Moore's house was painted by his daughter, Charlotte. The attention she gave to architectural details and to the texture of buildings and plant life indicate that she was an accomplished amateur painter, a reflection of her upbringing in the household of a well-educated man "called a philosopher."

Anson Pratt house (ca. 1802–12).
New Concord.

Historic American Building Survey records assign a building date of 1793 to this house. Other evidence, however, suggest a later date, sometime between 1802 and 1812. Anson Pratt (1771–1841) was born in Canaan, Connecticut. He first appears in public records in 1798 as the Chatham town clerk. He served in the state assembly in 1800, 1807, and 1810. There is no evidence that his parents were in this county, although other close relatives settled in the Kings District. It is possible that 1793 reflects the year Anson came to this region.

By 1800, when their first child was born at New Concord, Anson had married Sally Beebe, the daughter of Hosea Beebe, an early settler in that area. He may have obtained the land the house is built on from his father-in-law, who owned large but poorly identified tracts of land in the area. Precisely when Pratt came into possession of the land is not known. A town road list for 1801 assessed Anson Pratt for six days' work, only slightly above the average assessment for most of the 547 people listed. His elegant house would seem to reflect a greater wealth than was usual in New Concord. Besides his public service, other town and county records reveal that he held mortgages, acted as executor for estates, and dealt in land investments. He is said to have been in trade at New Concord, perhaps carrying on his father-in-law's store. The Pratt family history states that at New Concord he was a wealthy wool dealer. In such a capacity he would have been instrumental in Columbia County's first large-scale cloth manufacture, the first phase in the Industrial Revolution within the county *(p. 96)*. As a wool dealer, Anson Pratt may have acted as an agent between the wool-growers and the carding mill and between the carding mill and spinners and weavers. Finally he may have profited by taking the finished cloth to market. He is known to have owned a mill, but its type is not known.

Anson Pratt's years of public service and his apparent association with the mushrooming textile industry between 1802 and 1812 are factors that point toward this as a reasonable period of time during which the house might have been built.

The house, which is distinguished for its Adam-inspired detail, is closely related in type to houses surviving in the Berkshires and southward to Danbury, Connecticut, as well as to several others in Columbia County. At least two other houses in Columbia County are related to Anson Pratt's not only in architectural detail, but also in that their original owners had either a kinship or business connection with Pratt.

Anson Pratt House (detail)

The interior of this house is distinguished principally for a circular stairway rising in the middle of the house from cellar to third floor. Some of the mantels reflect exterior details, but otherwise the interior is restrained.

St. Peter's Presbyterian Church (1825). Route 203, Spencertown.

Spencertown was among the earliest New England settlements in Columbia County. By the 1750's this important community was established along the Great New England Road. As early as 1760, the proprietors resolved to erect a meeting house for religious purposes. Finally in 1771 one was built, and until 1824 the Congregational parish met here; in that year they placed themselves under the charge of the Columbia County Presbytery. In 1825 the church was moved a few feet west and "fitted up in modern style" to appear as it does today — a moderately large church executed in typical New England style of the Federal Period. For a time (1843–52) the Rev. Timothy Woodbridge, founder of the Spencertown Academy *(p. 105),* was pastor, and Sherman Griswold *(p. 129),* one of its parishioners. Reverend Woodbridge's father, also Timothy, of Williamstown, Massachusetts, had been instrumental in resolving the Massachusetts–New York border disputes during the 1770s.

Mills: The Beginning of the Industrial Revolution

Since at least 1661 the county's fast moving streams have made a significant contribution to the region's economy. Gristmills and sawmills have been in operation in the county for nearly three hundred years. Processing mills of many other types followed in the eighteenth century.

Early in the nineteenth century, America proclaimed its independence from European-made goods and entered the Industrial Revolution by building mills and plants for the manufacture of finished goods. The northeastern United States became the birthplace of America's Industrial Revolution. Columbia County's contribution included one of the first large-scale manufactures producing cloth on the water-powered looms at Columbiaville. This industry sprang up in other areas of the county, and in the nineteenth century woven and knit goods were the county's principal manufactured products.

Around 1790 the first carding machines were introduced to the United States. They saved hand spinners hours of time in the painstaking processing of picking over and preparing sheep fleece for spinning. Around 1800 Arthur Scholfield, one of the brothers who had built carding machines for New England use, set up a carding and loom operation at Pittsfield in adjacent Berkshire County, Massachusetts. This, combined with Robert R. Livingston's introduction of merino sheep in 1802, created favorable conditions for the emergence of an American textile industry. Until the fine-spun and fine-woven goods resulting from merino fleece appeared, woolen goods of American manufacture were coarse and unsuitable for fine clothing. By 1805 merino or merino half- and quarter-bred sheep were advertised in the Hudson *Bee*. In 1807 the breed was introduced into Berkshire County. The 1810 census reports that the town of Chatham manufactured 73,000 yards of wool and linen cloth a year. This was made on 138 family-owned looms.

Additionally three carding machines and four fulling mills (for finishing the surface of home-woven fabric) operated in the town.

Wool growing and weaving as a cottage industry remained an important part of Columbia County husbandry. In 1827 a convention dealing with the protection of the home manufacture of wool and the encouragement of the wool-growing industry met at Albany. The county was represented by the Federalists Elisha Williams, James Vanderpoel, and Jacob Rutsen Van Rensselaer. The first large-scale power loom operation in the state was at Columbiaville. Ironically it had been begun by anti-Federalists from Hudson. Although power looms supplanted cottage industry, sheep production and wool growing remained an important part of Columbia County's agriculture until late in the nineteenth century.

Penfield Map (detail, Henry Van Rensselaer's Mills). Collection of the Columbia County Historical Society.

Appearing at the left on this Claverack section of the Penfield map is the Van Rensselaer residence (p. 58). The center shows his fulling mills, sawmills, and gristmills, as well as the miller's house.

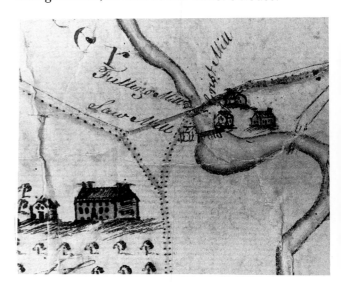

Humphriesville Mills (ca. 1767).
Photo collection, Rowles Studio, Hudson.

This gristmill is believed to have been built about 1767 by Henry Van Rensselaer *(p. 58)*. Daniel Penfield's map shows that in 1799 a complex of sawmills, gristmills, and fulling mills were operated at this site. In later years it was known as the Humphriesville Mills. Milling continued in the structure until it burned in 1926. This is the oldest mill in Columbia County of which a photograph exists.

Carroll Mill (ca. 1784)
built by James Nixon. Hudson.

The first of Hudson's industries was Peter Hogeboom's little mill, built before the New England proprietors purchased the site at Claverack Landing. On a nearby stream (probably near the site of Underhill Pond), Hogeboom's mill processed flour for local inhabitants. Because of inadequate water power, it was not very successful. Sometime after 1784, James Nixon, a Hudson proprietor, attempted to remedy the water problem by designing and building an extraordinarily large overshoot wheel. However, even delivering water by way of a tall, long aqueduct to the top of the wheel did not provide enough force to operate the mill. Although not the success he had hoped for, the mill is still a great testimony to an energetic and inventive approach to a difficult technical problem.

Penfield Map (detail, Barnard's Windmill).
Columbia County Historical Society.

Joseph Barnard, one of Hudson's New England proprietors, introduced the windmill to Columbia County. Although Hudson was surrounded by water power, since no good source of it was within the city limits, there resulted such inventive solutions as James Nixon's oversize water wheel and Joseph Barnard's windmill. Stephen Miller, Hudson's mid-nineteenth-century historian comments that the site must have provided ample power, but that carrying grist to the mill could have been an arduous task for the customers. Miller describes the mill:

The mill was octagonal in shape, two stories in height, built of heavy oak timber, sides shingled, and the wings which were very strongly constructed, were nearly seventy feet from the ground. In all approaches to the city it was a very prominent object and visible many miles distant.

The present Red Mills were begun by Jacob Rutsen Van Rensselaer probably around 1800, although some milling activity on this site existed during the eighteenth century. Gradually Van Rensselaer's mills became an important center for grain processing, and their capacity was enlarged to three hundred bushels of grain per day by the 1870s. In the middle of the nineteenth century plaster was also ground at the Red Mills. Grain and flour products were produced there until well into the twentieth century. At that time a steam engine was added to supplement the water wheel.

Red Mills (ca. 1800 with later additions). Route 23, Claverack.

View of Columbiaville (1907), oil on panel,
47⅞″ × 29⅞″, Gus Witzorek. Private Collection.

Near the middle of the county the Claverack and Kinderhook Creeks join to form the Stockport Creek. A sizable drop in the Stockport Creek, above its confluence with the Hudson River, afforded ample water for the development of a large mill complex in the early nineteenth century. In 1809 Robert Jenkins, Seth Macy, and other enterprising New Englanders from Hudson formed the Columbia Manufacturing Society and purchased the mill site at what is now Columbiaville. They contracted with Nathan Wild, an English machinist, for the construction of mills for the manufacture of cotton cloth. Then in 1824, James Wild built the mills on the south (left) side of the creek, and subsequently the Wild family assumed ownership of the operation. The large mill building built in 1824 on the south (left) side of the creek does not survive today. Architecturally it is nearly identical to the

mill at Stuyvesant Falls *(p. 101)*. The buildings on the north side of the creek were the original Columbia Manufacturing Society mill buildings, erected in 1812.

Farther upstream other cloth manufacturing mills were built. At nearby Stockport one of the first large-scale cloth printworks in the country was established by 1822; in 1826 it was owned by Benjamin and Joseph Marshall.

The wood bridge was built about 1792 with a king post truss. After it was built, the Post Road was rerouted. Going through Hudson shortened the mileage and thereby lowered the postal rates.

At least three painted versions of this view survive. The version shown here bears the inscription, "copied by Gus Witzorek, Columbiaville 1907/ original by Charles Walgust of Kinderhook in 1830." Another version, unsigned but believed to be an original, is owned by The American Museum in Britain. The only known information about the artists comes from the inscription.

Stuyvesant Falls Mills (1827, 1845). Stuyvesant Falls.

On the Kinderhook Creek three miles above its confluence with the Hudson River a precipitous drop totaling seventy feet became the power base for a complex of mills built during the nineteenth century. Known since 1823 as Stuyvesant Falls, the first known mills were constructed here about 1800 by Pitkin and Edmunds on the upper falls. About 1827 John and James Waddell built this five-story stone mill on the lower falls. In this mill eighty hands produced 325,000 yards of cotton cloth a year. In 1841 the Abraham A. Van Alen Co., which operated adjacent mills, absorbed the Waddell Mill and then in 1845 added a five-story brick mill just south of the stone one. Again, about 1873–88, they added a similar brick structure contiguous to the stone mill. At their height the Van Alen mills had 352 looms that produced 100,000 yards of cotton print cloth a week. At the end of the nineteenth century the Albany and Hudson Railroad and Power Company erected an electric generating plant powered by water for the purpose of providing power for the electric railroad then being built between Niverville and Hudson. The Van Alen mills at this time converted from water to electric power. Abraham Van Alen's daughter Anna acquired title to the mills, and they were operated by her husband Charles Frisbee as the Frisbee Mills until 1924. Since then the mills have been converted to other purposes including the manufacture of steel castings, batteries, and anesthetics and other medical gases.

These mills and the others that once existed around Stuyvesant Falls, producing paper, grist, plaster, and various cloths, are typical of those in a number of communities in Columbia County in the nineteenth century. It was an era of manufacturing of commercial products for the world outside the county. This contrasted to Columbia County in the seventeenth and eighteenth centuries when farming and farm product-related mills (grist, flour, lumber, fulling, etc.) dominated the county's economy.

Stuyvesant Falls mills — the existing mills and the sites of those demolished — is now a Historic District on the National Register of Historic Places.

The 1830s began a new era in Columbia County and, indeed, in the nation. Cultural values implicit in the experimental Federal Period had to be worked out. The inventiveness and resourcefulness of an optimistic new nation made full use of the opportunities the Industrial Revolution offered. Political, social, and technological changes were numerous and meaningful. Most important in Columbia County were the anti-rent wars (which caused the dissolution of the lease system of land ownership), the advent and expansion of railroads, and the industrial application of steam and other engines. These resulted in greater democracy, improved transportation to and from commercial and agricultural markets, and the growth of numerous small manufactories. This economic expansion changed the standard of living for many people; what had been the luxuries of the few landed aristocrats now were accessible to the mill owners, attorneys, farmers, merchants, and manufacturers. Education for all became possible. Good houses in a variety of styles were within the reach of the majority of people in the county, and art flourished in an atmosphere of prosperity.

The historic diversity of the period is apparent in its art and architecture. The variety of occupations possible for an individual increased, many of them requiring specialized training. Thus the roles of painters and housewrights changed. Beginning as students of painting and architecture, they were trained to be professional artists and architects. New social conditions gave them appreciative patrons and an economy that could support their work. Technology gave them portable paint in a tube (1840), photography, machine-tooled wood, and new building materials. The virtuosity of landscape painting and the richly varied architecture were the products of the American society.

III
In the American Tradition
1830s–1900

The Influence of Education

Americans valued education. By the 1830s classical training was widely available, and both public and private schools increased in number. The somewhat ornamental character of education emphasized in classical training introduced refined values to rural areas. One result, among others, was an increase in popular interest in art and architecture.

Clermont Academy (1834). Route 9, Clermont.

Clermont has the distinction of being the town in which the first public school in New York was established (by a special act of the New York legislature in 1791). Under the direction of Robert R. Livingston, Samuel Ten Broeck, and others, a school was built in Clermont from "monies in the hands of the overseers of the poor in the said town, arising from the excise and the fines which are not wanted for the relief of the poor. . . ."

Although that school building no longer survives, another school, the Clermont Academy, built as a high school in 1834, is located on a piece of land just a stone's throw away. When the 1791 school was demolished in 1855, the academy building became a public school and more recently a community center. Clermont academy was founded in 1834 at a meeting of the inhabitants of the town wherein Edward P. Livingston proposed the following resolution for its establishment:

Whereas we are sensibly impressed with tendency of education to improve the moral and social condition of men, as well as its advantages in enabling them to appreciate the blessings of civil and religious liberty, and to fulfill the duties of those stations to which, as citizens of a free government they may be called: therefore resolve. . . .

The Academy building was completed that year by the contractor Philip S. Staats for under $1500 on a lot donated by Edward P. Livingston.

The minutes of the board of trustees describe the building as finished with cupola, belfry, and lightning rod, painted white, enclosed by a board fence, and planted with ornamental trees. Built for "durability and convenience," the lower floor was divided into two schoolrooms and a hall; the upper floor was fitted up as a chapel for religious exercises.

The Federal style architecture of the academy is a conservative holdover in an era that usually embraced the Greek Revival style for its public buildings.

Spencertown Academy (1847). Route 203, Spencertown.

Spencertown Academy had its origins in the educational philosophies prevalent in the first half of the nineteenth century and also in the enthusiasms and devotion of the Reverend Timothy Woodbridge (1787–1862). Prior to his service in Spencertown Presbyterian Church, Woodbridge was a minister at nearby Green River, where he also took a great interest in bringing education to the whole community. He began a classical school there and erected an "elegant edifice" called the Green River Academy, which had from forty to sixty pupils during its early years. In 1842 after twenty-six years at Green River, he moved to Spencertown. In 1845 he addressed himself to the needs for education in that community. In order to obtain funds from the state, a portion of money had to be raised locally for the building of a school. Benjamin Ambler, a Spencertown resident, amazed everyone by raising several thousand dollars in only a few days. In Woodbridge's *Autobiography of a Blind Minister,* he tells that Benjamin Ambler was then contracted to build the "noble structure with his accustomed fidelity and good taste. Mr. A. is a mason by trade, and a distinguished housebuilder; but he has a great soul, which would qualify him to build a nobler edifice than a fine house. He has a mind enough to build the moral structure of a State. . . ." The academy was finished in 1847. Its rather late use of Greek Revival style was probably inspired by Woodbridge's commitment to classical education for both boys and girls. It continued in use as a school until 1972, when it became a community center maintained by the Spencertown Academy Association.

Claverack College and Hudson River Institute (1854).
Route 9H, Claverack.
Columbia County Historical Society Collections.

What became the major educational institution in Columbia County in the late nineteenth century, began in 1777 as Washington Seminary established by the Reverend Gabriel Gebhard. It was here that the versatile and prominent educator Andrew Mayfield Carshore supervised the education of various Federal Period leaders *(see pp. 65,67,68).* By 1830 the demand for a school of expanded curriculum resulted in the school's becoming an academy with a new building erected by Colonel Ambrose Root. In 1854 the academy was again re-chartered as the Claverack College and Hudson River Institute at which young men were prepared for the junior class in college. The new curriculum included instruction in eleven departments — classical, French, German, English, normal, musical,

painting, military, commercial, telegraphic, and agricultural. After 1869 there was also a collegiate course for women.

The four-story main building contained 146 student rooms, 13 teachers' rooms, 12 lecture and recitation halls, 28 music rooms, society and reading rooms, a library, chapel, office, and 35 rooms for domestic uses of the institute. In addition on the twenty-acre grounds were an armory, drill house, and gymnasium. Throughout its history the school was closely associated with the Reformed Church at Claverack, and its minister was usually the head of the school.

The 1831 section was, like the Clermont Academy, a late example of Federal architecture. When Claverack College was expanded in 1854, the new structure was the largest and probably the last Greek Revival structure in Columbia County. The College closed in 1902, and the building was torn down shortly thereafter.

The initial growth of the city of Hudson gradually halted with the Embargo of 1807 and the War of 1812. A general economic failure in 1819 put the city into decline. But in 1830 a handful of hopeful citizens began to revive the city's economy with the formation of a new whaling company. Their success in the enterprise was infectious, and Hudson began to grow and to build again. The river continued as the chief source of the city's economy. Even as the burst of its second success leveled off, Hudson remained Columbia County's political, commercial, and industrial center in the midst of an agricultural region.

In 1805 the county seat was transferred from Claverack to Hudson, but not without much opposition in the countryside against the increasing preeminence of the new Quaker city. Hudson's City Hall became the courthouse, and, as usual, a jail was attached. This structure survives at 364 Warren Street and has been occupied for over a century by the *Hudson-Register Star* and its parent newspapers.

The courthouse is a straightforward example of the Greek Revival style based on the Greek temple form. Although the Greek temple form was newly fashionable in residential architecture, precedent for its use in public buildings went back to Benjamin Latrobe's introduction of it in 1798. Its appeal was partly political, for the United States' national identity early associated itself with the ancient Greek democratic ideals. During the Greek struggle for independence in the 1820s this association was intensified and led to the widespread adoption of Greek architectural forms. The aesthetic appeal of these forms was also great because the impressive formal proportions could be scaled to any size building.

The third courthouse was demolished in 1900 to be replaced by a similar but larger structure (*p. 156*), which burned in 1907 and was replaced by the present courthouse, also of classical inspiration.

Third County Courthouse (1835), photograph (ca. 1860) by Frank Forshew, Hudson. Courtesy Rowles Studio, Hudson.

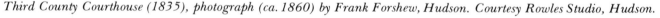

Weathervane (before 1835), First Presbyterian Church.
Hudson, New York.

Broadside soliciting bids for the construction
of the third courthouse (1834).
Collections of Columbia County Historical Society.

This vane has been in this position since 1835–37, when the present church building was erected. It was moved here from the first building of the Presbyterian congregation, built in 1792. It is not known if the vane might have been on the first building since 1792.

The new church was erected on three lots on Warren Street, at the site of the old courthouse. In addition to the traditional function of indicating prevailing winds for the information of farmers and planters, prominent urban vanes like this may have been a source of interest to sailors' families anticipating the arrival or departure of sloops and sea-going sailing vessels from the port of Hudson.

In 1833 a committee of three supervisors was appointed to review proposals for the erection of a new courthouse. The economic revival of Hudson during the 1830s had awakened civic pride in Hud- son, and popular interest in public buildings and in the general appearance of the city grew. Finally plans for the building were drawn by Henry Rec- tor, an architect active in Albany during the 1830s and 1840s. Three firms bid for the construction of the building, and the contract was awarded to Burch, King, and Waterman, the latter possibly the noted builder Barnabus Waterman (or his son) who had built other structures in or near Hudson.

"The Whale Ship Beaver *of Hudson" (1840), watercolor on paper, 18¼" × 25", Isaac Power. Private collection.*

Between 1830 and 1845 up to fourteen ships of the newly formed Hudson Whaling Company regularly sailed out of Hudson in the successful pursuit of whales around the globe. One of the ships of this company was the *Beaver,* which had been purchased in 1832 by Messrs. Barnard and Curtiss of Hudson *(pp. 110 and 111)* from John Jacob Astor. The captain was Jared Gardner (b. 1768) originally of Nantucket, who was said to have sailed for Astor in the fur trade before sailing for the Hudson whale fishery. The voyage depicted in this watercolor commenced in 1832 with the *Beaver* returning to Hudson in 1836 with 1900 barrels of sperm oil. Hudson's whaling effort came to a halt in 1845 along with a general decline in the industry. Shortly thereafter Hudson's third economic period began when it became the first terminous on the Hudson River of a railroad line from the east coast.

Isaac Power was a son of an early Hudson settler, Thomas Power. Although no record of an artist's career has come to light, there is a sketch of another Thomas Power, perhaps a brother or a cousin, which may also be by Isaac. Presumably he was a crew member on the *Beaver.* Significantly, although there are records of land transactions by Isaac Power in Hudson over many years, there are none listed for 1826 to 1837, years in which the *Beaver* was at sea. His spirited depiction of the dangers and excitement of whaling is the only known picture of one of Hudson's whaling ships. The painting is inscribed "Near the Galapagos Islands in 1833/drawn and painted by Isaac Power 1840."

Cyrus Curtiss house (ca. 1834–37; wing ca. 1870). 32 Warren Street, Hudson.

From its founding by a group of New England merchants and shippers in 1786, Hudson grew rapidly. Although it was 130 miles from the sea, Hudson's prosperity was founded on shipping and all the ancillary manufactories that went with it: shipbuilding, sailmaking, and oil and candle works. Lumber, hoops, staves, fish, and farm produce were shipped from Hudson to points all over the coast, especially to southern ports. Whaling ships returned with oil and whale bone. Goods of all kinds were imported from Europe and the Orient. Cyrus Curtiss, co-owner of the *Beaver*, began a large oil and candle works in the 1830s in partnership with Mr. Barnard. It soon became one of the largest such manufactories in the country. This may have been the basis for his building such a substantial home on Warren Street about this time. Shortly after its construction, in 1837, Curtiss sold this house to Seneca Butts. The sale may have been connected either with a personal tragedy (his business is known to have twice burned down) or with the general economic panic of 1837. Some years later (1844) Curtiss was elected mayor of Hudson for two years. It was during his tenure that the tenants' rebellion known as the anti-rent wars became especially heated in Columbia County. Curtiss was forced to issue a proclamation calling for five hundred "Minute Men" to defend Hudson from a threatened burning by the tenants on the adjacent Livingston Manor. So unpopular was the manorial system by then that the New York legislature abolished it in 1846.

Greek Revival houses came in different forms, though they all shared a number of details inspired by Greek architecture. Many such houses have a "Greek temple" appearance with pediment and columns facing the front. The Curtiss house, however, is a variant on the Greek Revival style, the facade being flat, like a peristyle, surmounted by a nearly flat roof on which is found an octagonal cupola from which all of Hudson and the South Bay could be seen. Five elaborate scrollwork grilles, covering windows in the frieze, admit light to the attic. Above the door a similar grille covers the transom window. A pair of Doric columns flank the door, and another pair of larger but similar columns support the porch — all painted white in imitation of the white marble of the original Greek temples. Columned porticos similar to this one were often added to older houses in the county as a fashionable renovation.

A fire destroyed Barnard and Curtiss' sperm oil and candle factory in 1839. They built a new works, illustrated here, with fireproof brick and furnished it with all new machinery. The result was the most modern factory of its type in Hudson.

The illustrator Throop is likely one of three brothers, John P. V. N. (1794–ca. 1861), Orramel H. (1798–n.d.), or Daniel S. (1800–n.d.), who were born at Oxford, New York, but connected with a Columbia County family. The three had careers as illustrators. The best known is John Peter Van Ness Throop, who worked in Washington, D.C., as an illustrator, engraver, medallist, and miniaturist. As namesake of Washington's mayor *(page 68)*, he may have benefited as a result. The other two brothers are known to have worked in New York State.

Only a few volumes of the *Rural Repository,* a literary journal published in Hudson, contained illustrations, suggesting that such art was not regularly available.

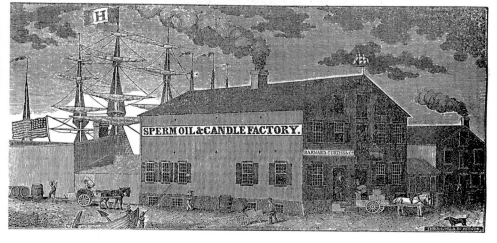

Sperm Oil & Candle Factory, Hudson (1841), engraving, Throop.
Published in the Rural Repository.
Collection of Columbia County Historical Society.

The steamboat Nuhpa of Hudson
(ca. 1865), oil on canvas, James Bard.
Courtesy Rowles Studio, Hudson.

The *Nuhpa* actually began life in 1863 as the *Berkshire* and ran as a passenger boat between Hudson and New York City. In 1864 the *Berkshire* partially burned and was rebuilt a year later with a stern propeller by J. S. Baldwin at New Baltimore. Renamed the *Nuhpa*, it was 1231 gross tons, 253 feel long, with a 37-foot beam and 10-foot draft. The engine was built with a single piston (as were most in those days) of 37-inch diameter with a 5-foot stroke.

James Bard (1815–97) and his twin brother, John, (1815–56) were the best known and most prolific marine artists to record the steamboats that plied the Hudson River in the great age of steam. Nowhere else in the world did the speed and elegance of steamboats reach the heights it did on this river in the nineteenth century.

This view of the *Nuhpa* is taken from a glass negative made by Frank Forshew of Hudson *(see p. 115)* of the original painting whose present location is not known.

This advertisement in the 1868 *Hudson Directory* shows a woodcut of the *Nuhpa* copied from the Bard painting. The *Nuhpa*, as the ad indicates, made regular night runs between Hudson and Albany on the Hudson River. Its captain, F. M. Power, came from a family of Hudson settlers who were involved in whaling *(see p. 109)* and in the ferry service between Hudson and Athens. In later years the *Nuhpa* was renamed the *Metropolitan*. It was broken up in 1897.

Woodcut prints such as this enlivened advertisements for products and services in mid-nineteenth-century newspapers and city directories.

The General Worth Hotel (1838).
Formerly at 215 Warren Street, Hudson.

When a fire destroyed an earlier hotel on this site, it took just one hundred days to build a new one. The Hudson House as it was first called by the stock company that erected it in 1838, catered to travelers and merchants who transferred at Hudson from riverboats to stagecoaches for the trip inland towards the popular resorts—northwest to Lebanon Springs and the Berkshires or south to New York City. Frequent visitors to Lebanon Springs and the nearby Shaker community stopped at the Hudson House on their way. In later years it was called Bagley's Hotel, then the Worth House and the General Worth Hotel (in honor of William Jenkins Worth, a Hudson native and Mexican War hero). At one time in the nineteenth century Hudson was so active that as many as two hundred travelers might stop here in a day. In

recent years business dwindled until the Miller family, who had owned it for over a century, closed its doors. Abandoned and deteriorating, it was demolished in 1969, but not without a spirited campaign by historic preservationists to save this rare example of an urban hotel.

When it was built in 1838, it was patterned after the Tremont House of Boston (constructed in 1828–29 by architect Isaiah Rogers), the first "modern" urban hotel in America. Unlike eighteenth-century inns, which were basically converted residences, the new hotel was designed specifically for this function. Its public rooms were on the first floor, and the upper floors were composed of banks of rooms along straight corridors.

The exterior of the hotel was a fine example of urban Greek Revival design with a scale and dignity that accurately reflected the prosperity of a town that deserved a "modern" hotel comparable to the newest ones in New York City and Boston.

Batchellor's Bazaar, 120 Warren Street, Hudson. Photograph (ca. 1868), by Frank Forshew. Courtesy Rowles Studio, Hudson.

In 1868, James Batchellor advertised his new store at 120 Warren Street, illustrated in Forshew's photograph. As early as 1858 he had operated the Bazaar at 124 Warren Street, the frame building shown at the extreme right in the photograph. That building was said to have been the one used by Erastus Pratt for his business in 1798.

Forshew's photograph is a useful record of late eighteenth- and early nineteenth-century buildings on lower Warren Street. In spite of the later alterations at street level, the appearance of early nineteenth-century Hudson is also conveyed, for few architectural changes were made on the upper parts of the buildings.

The advent of photography in the 1840s altered the role of the painter. As this photograph testifies, sign painting was still important, but no painter had ever endeavored a cityscape such as Frank Forshew made. Besides being an excellent record of the scene, it includes many details of human interest.

Forshew was the son of John Forshew who left Stonington, Connecticut, as a sea captain and lost everything in a shipwreck. He began anew in Hudson as a school teacher. His son Frank, born in 1827, pioneered in Hudson with a daguerrotype business in 1849. In 1865 he erected the brick block that bore his name. He took a considerable interest in civic affairs — an interest preserved in the numerous photographs he took of Hudson and the environs during the last half of the nineteenth century.

Laying cobblestones on upper Warren Street, Hudson.
Photograph (ca. 1868), Frank Forshew.
Courtesy Rowles Studio, Hudson.

The Greek Revival

The Greek Revival style of architecture achieved greater popularity in America than anywhere else. Although first introduced in the late eighteenth century, it became popular in the 1820s as major public buildings, such as Jefferson's design for the University of Virginia, were constructed in this style. For the next twenty years the architecture of the world's first democracy became the preferred style of Jacksonian era democracy. Not only in the East but throughout the newly settled Midwest (Ohio, Indiana, Illinois, and Michigan), houses in the form of Greek temples, or similar adaptations, symbolized the aesthetic and political values of a newly expansionist country.

Loren Van Valkenberg house (ca. 1843). Albany Turnpike, Malden Bridge.

In 1843, Loren Van Valkenburgh purchased from his parents part of a large tract, including a wagon and blacksmith shop and residence. Some surviving interior materials suggest that the wing of this house is older than the Greek Revival section. The building date of the house is unknown, but since the premises had not been occupied by the immediate family before Loren owned the property and since such Greek Revival styles were popular in the county in the 1840s *(see Spencertown Academy p. 105)*, Loren Van Valkenburg's purchase date probably reflects the time at which the extensive Greek Revival alterations and additions were made. Loren maintained a store and post office at this site until he and his third wife sold the property in 1862. Owners in the later nineteenth century made additional improvements.

The Van Valkenburgh house is a typical interpretation of the Greek Revival style in Columbia County. The simplified capitals on the columns and the severe treatment of doorway jambs and lintel are one kind of interpretation made by talented local housewrights who chose from carpenters' pattern books (like Minard Lafever's *The Modern Builder's Guide* [1833]) that illustrated elevations, floor plans, mouldings, doors, windows, mantels, and other decorative details of Greek Revival fashion. The local builder who adapted or copied these designs produced for his client an individual variant adapted to local taste and circumstance.

Uel Lawrence house (ca. 1845–50). South Street, Spencertown.

The date of erection of this remarkable Greek Revival house has been confused by a historical marker identifying it as the Elisha Williams house. Although Williams (1773–1833) began his legal career in Spencertown and continued to own property there, he moved to Hudson around 1800 and remained there and in New York City until his death. Although Greek elements had been introduced into American buildings in the eighteenth century, it was not until 1817, when Thomas Jefferson designed the imitation temples for the University of Virginia (erected 1823), that the temple form became popular. Even then, it was not until 1830 that it was adapted for dwelling use and popularized in 1833 by Minard Lafever's *Modern Builders Guide.*

Uel Lawrence and his brother George were sons of an early Spencertown settler, Judah Monis Lawrence. Both sons were active in local and county affairs and held several elected positions in the nineteenth century. Both built fine Greek revival style houses directly across the road from each other. George's house was of fine proportions with details rendered in the simpler Doric order. Uel chose the somewhat more elaborate Ionic order, readily identified by its scrolled capitals.

The building date of the house is not known, but sometime between 1845 and about 1850 is most likely. In 1845 Uel purchased from his brother large tracts of land in this vicinity formerly owned by the heirs of John Griswold. In 1862 he sold the house with a one-and-one-fourth acre lot and moved across the road. The presence in Spencertown of an accomplished Greek Revival style builder and the Lawrence brothers' membership on the Spencertown Academy building committee suggest a relationship between the buildings. According to Franklin Ellis' county history, the building committee drew up the plans for the Academy, which was then built by Benjamin Ambler (*see p. 105*). Somewhat contradictory to the Ellis account is that of the Academy's founder, Timothy Woodbridge, who credits Ambler with the design of the building. The imposing monumentality of this house calls to mind Woodbridge's high praise for Ambler.

The porticoed facade creates the symmetry and compactness that characterize the Greek temple style. Careful attention to such proportions as the diameter of the columns in relation to their height and the height of the pediment in relation to the portico produce a form that can be scaled to any size. Unusual in Columbia County is the highly ornamental architrave, which is carried around the house under the eaves. Other decorative mouldings on the exterior add further elegance, making this perhaps the finest example of the Greek Revival style in the county.

Mantel (ca. 1830s), Finger Road, Greenport.

In many cases, as new styles become fashionable, earlier features were replaced by more modern ones. In this instance, a mantel whose form is associated with Greek Revival architecture replaced an earlier Federal one. The free-standing columns replicate the columns on many Greek Revival houses.

Within the three panels on this mantel are small oil paintings, a unique ornamentation. One is signed "C. Baker 1875," presumably Charles Baker (1839–88), a New York landscape painter who must have visited this home to paint these scenes of sunrise, moonlight, and an unidentified lake.

Art in Columbia County came into its own in the 1830s. Itinerant, native-born, and resident painters made a place for themselves in county life. Portraits continued to be popular, but they were produced in a wider variety of styles than formerly. New subject matter, such as landscapes, still lifes, and architectural paintings, became important. Newly educated and prosperous Americans wanted to have and were able to afford art as never before.

Portrait of Luman Reed (ca. 1830), oil on canvas, 30⅛" × 25⅜", Asher B. Durand. Courtesy The Metropolitan Museum of Art. Bequest of Mary Fuller Wilson, 1963.

Luman Reed (1785–1836) was born at Green River in Columbia County. As a boy, he moved with his family to Catskill where the father, and later the son, engaged in business as a merchant along the river. Luman Reed's business expanded, and he moved to New York, where he also became a patron of the arts. Not only did he assemble a collection of works by then-modern landscape painters like Thomas Cole (1801–48) and Asher B. Durand (1796–1886), but his generous commissions to these young artists enabled them to make a living painting landscape instead of the heretofore profitable portraits. His patronage greatly aided the establishment of the Hudson River school of painting. Reed himself, the artists he supported, and their work all reflect the democratic atmosphere in which a new kind of American art flourished.

Asher B. Durand's career began in engraving; during the 1820s he was America's foremost engraver. His painting career began with portraiture, but gradually he switched his attention to landscapes. In 1840–41 he traveled with Francis W. Edmunds *(p. 128)* to the art centers of Europe. Later he served as president of the National Academy of Design (1845–61.)

Lauriette Ashley (ca. 1828), oil on canvas, 70" × 50⅝",
Erastus Salisbury Field.
Courtesy The St. Louis Art Museum.
Gift of Mrs. James H. Spencer.

In the late eighteenth century William Ashley came from Amherst, Massachusetts, to Hudson and obtained land at Windmill Hill (see p. 98). As its first resident, he renamed it Prospect Hill. The community that grew up there was called Unionville; in 1807 when the new Hudson Academy was built there, the name of the hill was again changed, this time to Academy Hill (see p. 73). Lauriette (1803–70) was the only daughter of William Ashley and his second wife and was remembered by relatives as an individual of serious purpose, devoted to her church and the abolitionist cause. The descendant who gave the painting to the St. Louis Art Museum believed that it had been painted by one of her admirers.

The painter was her first cousin, Erastus Salisbury Field (1805–1900), William Ashley's nephew, from Leverett, Massachusetts. Field had studied briefly in New York City with Samuel F. B. Morse until Morse left the city. His career spanned about seventy years (1822–90) and included not only portraiture, but creative photography and biblical, classical, and historical paintings as well. From 1825 to 1840 he traveled in New York and New England, producing portraits in provincial style. In 1828 he was in Hudson and wrote a letter to his father, saying that he found his work accepted and would "tarry there as long as I can obtain business. . . ." The portrait of Lauriette Ashley is his first known life-size, full-length work. The house in the landscape may be Lauriette's own home.

Lauriette died in 1870 at the home of her half sister, Mary Ashley Van Alstyne, in Schodack Landing. During her lifetime the portrait was never framed and had been stored rolled up.

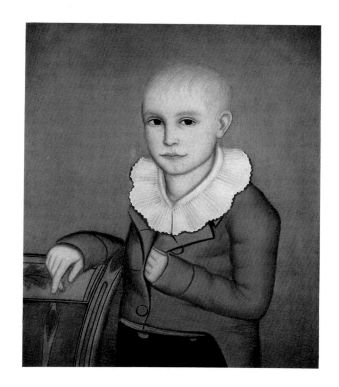

Russell Griffin Dorr (ca.1814), oil on canvas,
24⅝" × 20", Ammi Phillips.
Courtesy Abby Aldrich Rockefeller Folk Art Collection

Russell G. Dorr was one of the nine members of the Dr. Russell Dorr family of Chatham Center who were portrayed by Ammi Phillips about 1814. Today the nine portraits survive, some still owned by descendants and others by museums. There is evidence that Phillips painted the portraits of other complete families in the county (*see p. 122*).

Although Russell G. Dorr's parents came from New England, they lived at Chatham Center. Besides practicing medicine, Dr. Dorr has been credited with the invention of an early threshing machine.

His son, Russell, Jr., grew up and married Harriet Park in 1832. Her family was at Hillsdale, where the young couple lived, and Russell G. Dorr began practice as one of the earliest lawyers in that town. One of his clients was the Harlem Railroad, which went through Hillsdale. But of greater interest is the role he came to play in the anti-rent struggles of the 1840s. These disputes had their roots in the manor landholding system of the colonial period. Most evidence indicates that in the eighteenth-century tenants lived on comfortable terms with manor lords and that they had an opportunity to share in the profits of their labor. Protests against the manor system in the eighteenth century stemmed from New Englanders' challenge to the right of New Yorkers to own the land at all. While primogeniture and entail were abolished by the legislature in 1782, the tenant-rent system was retained to the benefit of numerous landed Hudson valley families.

The anti-rent movement came on the heels of widespread economic upheaval resulting from the Panic of 1837 and the subsequent death of the third Stephen Van Rensselaer, the "Good" patroon in January 1839. According to his will, debts of his estate were to be paid by the collection of rents in arrear. Thus anti-rent opposition began with the Van Rensselaer holdings. Tenants of other large landholders like the Van Cortland, Hardenbergh, Verplank, and Livingston families caught the spirit of the democratic rebellion. As these actions took place the real meaning of Jacksonian democracy hit the Hudson valley. In towns of southern Columbia County that were still part of Livingston and Van Rensselaer holdings, farmers — often descendants of early settlers — joined the anti-rent cause. The events culminated in 1844–45.

By this time Russell G. Dorr was a supreme court commissioner in Hillsdale. He was sympathetic to the anti-rent cause though not active in it. In January 1845, Dr. Boughton, the great anti-rent movement leader, was jailed in Hudson; and the city became embroiled in the controversy. Boughton's lawyers secured from Dorr an order directing Sherriff Miller of Hudson to bring Dr. Boughton to Hillsdale for a hearing, and Dorr was reputed to be part of a plot to rescue Boughton at Hillsdale. As a result, Governor Silas Wright sent John Van Buren to remove Dorr from his position as commissioner. Shortly after this occasion, Dorr's commitment to the cause became stronger, and he spoke to a meeting of anti-renters at Churchtown, demanding just, humanitarian administration of the law.

*The Ten Broeck Twins,
Jacob W. (left)
and William H. (1834),
oil on canvas
Ammi Phillips
Collection of Mrs. J.
Wessel Ten Broeck.*

*Jacob Wessel and
William Henry
Ten Broeck (ca. 1880),
charcoal on paper,
24" × 20".
Collection of
Dr. and Mrs. Roderic
H. Blackburn.*

*Sarah Ann and
Mary Jane Evarts
Ten Broeck (ca. 1880),
charcoal on paper,
24" × 20".
Collection of
Dr. and Mrs. Roderic
H. Blackburn.*

Adeline Foster Bain (ca.1833), oil on panel, 32⅝" × 30¼", attributed to Ira C. Goodell. Columbia County Historical Society. Gift of Mrs. John W. D. Hyndman, 1932.

The Ten Broeck twins were born at the homestead farm in Germantown that their great-great grandfather had purchased from the first Robert Livingston in 1694 *(see p. 40)*. To Jacob W., the twin on the left, descended an early New York portrait of the first Jacob Ten Broeck (one of Dirck Wessels Ten Broeck's sons) and the great family Bible. The twins' father and mother, Jacob and Anna Benner Ten Broeck, moved from the Clermont farm to one in Greenport in 1844. Each of the twins was given one of the farms, and in 1846 the parents moved to the city of Hudson. There the twins' father was director of the Farmers' Bank of Hudson and active in state and local politics; he was elected assemblyman in 1862 and was mayor of Hudson during the troubled years of the Civil War (1863–64). In 1847 and 1848 William (1823–88) and Jacob (1823–96) married, respectively, Mary Jane and Sarah Ann, twin daughters of Jacob and Gertrude Evarts.

Since the boys were born on April 22, 1823, and Phillips has inscribed the reverse of the portrait with their age (ten years) in 1834, the painting can be attributed to the winter or early spring of 1834, while Phillips (1788–1865) was still living in nearby Rhinebeck, Dutchess County. Phillips' portraits of the parents and a brother, Andrew Jackson Ten Broeck, also survive. Three sisters were also part of the family and may have had their portraits taken at this time. Soon after this, Ammi Phillips and his family moved to Amenia, New York, eastward but still close to Columbia County's southern border; yet Columbia County portraits from his later career are not known. It may be that other resident artists in the county succeeded in filling local needs.

The finely drawn portraits of the Ten Broeck twins and the twin sisters they married mark the influence of photography as well as the changing styles of portraiture in the second half of the nineteenth century.

The portraitist whose work was signed I. Goodell or I. G. Goodell has been identified by Cynthia Seibels (of the Abby Aldrich Rockefeller Folk Art Collection) as Ira Chaffee Goodell, born in 1800 in Belchertown, Massachusetts. During the 1820s, Goodell worked in central Massachusetts. Later he moved to New York, from approximately 1832 through 1834 he was active in Columbia and adjacent counties. Records place him in New York City subsequently. He returned to Belchertown after 1871 and died within a few years. More than twenty of his portraits of locally prominent Columbia County residents indicate that Goodell painted widely in the county — at Malden Bridge, Spencertown, Hillsdale, Kinderhook, Claverack, Hudson, and Columbiaville. Like Ammi Phillips he worked in more than one style. Goodell's early portraits are flat, one-dimensional paintings with strong emphasis on design. In the Columbia County portraits of the 1830s, Goodell usually combined decorative costume details and more realistic modelling of faces.

Adeline Foster Bain was the only child of Isaac Foster and his first wife, Lucy. She was also the granddaughter of Parla Foster, a Revolutionary soldier who prospered in Hillsdale after the war. The substantial brick mansion he built stands today at the intersection of Routes 22 and 23 in Hillsdale.

James E. Delamater (1838), oil on canvas,
36" × 30", Henry F. Prime.
Collection of Dr. and Mrs. Roderic H. Blackburn.

James E. Delamater advertised his "tasteful and elegant" carriages in newspapers and with this card, produced by a Hudson engraver named Throop. He himself executed the ornamental painting which decorated the carriages.

James E. Delamater's business card (1844), 2½" × 3¾".
Collection of Dr. and Mrs. Roderic H. Blackburn.

James Elting Delamater (1808–ca. 1850) was born on the family farm southwest of Hudson. In 1830, in partnership with William Heermance, he purchased a Hudson wagon-making shop. Two years later he bought his partner's half and expanded the shop into a large manufactory of several buildings for the production of carriages and sleighs. Several men and apprentices worked in the carriage plant, specializing in the blacksmithing and woodworking skills needed to make the carriages. In 1838 Delamater married Catherine Bronck. She died in 1841, and in 1843 he married Caroline Storm of Mellenville.

On April 10, 1845 *The Hudson Washingtonian* reported that Delamater's entire manufactory had burned to the ground, representing a loss of between $12,000 and $14,000.

Delamater's portrait is inscribed on the reverse "H. F. Prime/1838." Henry F. Prime (ca. 1811–1841) had worked in Troy as a portrait painter in 1834. With his wife Ann Maria and their three children, he lived in Hudson from 1838 or earlier until his death in 1841. He is said to have executed many portraits during the period in Hudson, and he exhibited in 1839 and 1840 at the National Academy in New York City. He appears to be related to an Albany family of painters and craftsmen of the same name who worked in Albany, Troy, and Hudson from the 1830s to the 1850s.

Catskill, New York (1849), oil on canvas, 34" × 44", Albertus del Orient Browere. Collections The Brooklyn Museum.

The view of Catskill was taken from Columbia County. Many painters must have come to the county to paint the Catskill Mountains, which are best seen from the east side of the Hudson River. Browere's foreground is located in the vicinity of the town line between Greenport and Livingston. Browere's subjects are often rural genre scenes: in this painting he combines landscape elements with genre details, providing a view of the village of Catskill, river transportation, vernacular architecture, and daily life. Like Henry Ary, Browere gives considerable attention to botanical detail. Although

no formal relationships have been established between the two, it may be that both of these painters developed this trait as a result of knowledge of Thomas Cole's work and its praise of the American forest.

Browere was born at Tarrytown and pursued a painting career, exhibiting in New York City in 1832. In 1834 he moved to Catskill, New York, where he remained until the 1850s, when he traveled twice to California. Hudson valley legend and landscape are the subject of most of his paintings.

Scene on the Hudson River (ca. 1850), oil on canvas, 25 13/16" × 36", Henry Ary.
The Brooklyn Museum, Dick S. Ramsay Fund.

This Hudson River scene appears to be taken from behind Mt. Merino, looking northwesterly with the village of Athens on the left and a glimpse of Hudson on the extreme right. Henry Ary (ca. 1807–59) painted Mt. Merino many times and from a variety of angles. The hill dominates Hudson's landscape and received its name from the Spanish breed of sheep introduced to the country by Robert Livingston in 1807. During the following decade a large flock of merinos was raised on a farm that later became known as the Wiswall farm. Oliver Wiswall was a mayor of Hudson, and it is the roof-

top of his house that is seen on the left edge of the hill.

Henry Ary was born in Rhode Island in ca. 1807. Nothing is known of his early life until 1831 and 1832 when he was listed in an Albany directory as a portrait painter at a State Street studio very near to Ezra Ames's. According to Durand's obituary in the *Crayon*, Ary spent some time in Catskill before coming to Hudson around 1844. Until his death he lived in Hudson, painting portraits and landscapes, sometimes working on special commissions for various patrons and selling landscapes through the American Art Union. For the city of Hudson he painted a full length portrait of George Washington, more than seven and a half feet high, a copy of the Lansdowne portrait of Washington by Gilbert Stuart.

In this work Henry Ary (ca. 1807–59) develops themes traditional to the early landscape painters: detailed rendering of small plants and trees give texture and variety to the landscape; and elaborate cloud formations dramatize the sky. In the midst of natural grandeur elements of human endeavor are minutely characterized. The city of Hudson, although occupying only a small part of the landscape, is presented in great detail. Ary's panoramic view of Hudson is an unusual record of town and landscape. Most of the larger buildings are identifiable, and some still stand today.

View of the City of Hudson (1852), oil on canvas, 26" × 36", Henry Ary.
Courtesy the Albany Institute of History and Art.

The Scythe Grinder (1856), oil on canvas, 42" × 33", Francis W. Edmunds. Courtesy The New-York Historical Society.

The son of an early settler, Francis William Edmunds (1806–63) was born and raised in Hudson. At an early age Francis showed a talent for drawing; his first drawing was of a soldier on horseback during an 1812 recruiting rendezvous in Hudson. At fifteen he sought apprenticeship with an engraver; but the fee was too high, and he took a job in his uncle's bank in New York. He continued his interest in art, leading a dual life as a bank cashier and, under a pseudonym, exhibiting (by 1836) at the National Academy of Design. His subject matter was the common man and everyday life.

He and William Sidney Mount of Long Island became the leading genre painters in America. Of the two, some contemporaries felt that Edmunds pos-sessed greater talent but that not pursu-ing art full time diminished his stand-ing in the art world. At the end of an extended tour of European art centers in 1840 and 1841, he wrote of his deci-sion to "paint little and rather for pleas-ure than reputation." Yet in the fol-lowing years his art remained an im-portant part of his life. His public career not only involved banking but also politics, election as vice president of the New York Gallery of Fine Arts, an active membership in the American Art Union, and membership in the Na-tional Academy.

The Scythe Grinder survives in three forms. An oil study for this painting is privately owned and was made pre-paratory to the finished work. This painting served as the model from which an engraving for the American Bank Note Company was made. Ed-monds was an officer and director of that company, as well as its resident ar-tist.

The Reverend Cyrus Stebbins (ca. 1830), oil on canvas, 26⅝" × 21", unidentified artist. Courtesy Christ Church, Hudson.

Born in Massachusetts, Cyrus Steb-bins (1772–1841) began his ministerial services as a Methodist preacher in Al-bany. His views changed, however, and he later joined the Episcopal clergy. In 1819 he came to the Christ Church parish in Hudson and served there until 1832, the longest ministry at that church during the nineteenth century. The congregation had been formed about 1790, and the Hudson city pro-prietors had provided a lot for the church, which was finally erected in 1802. It was not until 1820 that its spire was completed and a new bell hung there in 1823. Stebbins is said to have been instrumental in implementing this building program. During the years 1854–57, the parish undertook the building of a new house of worship, that serves the congregation today *(see p. 135)*.

Following his long service to Christ Church, Stebbins went to Waterford, New York, where he died 1841. Since the portrait is in the possession of the church, it seems reasonable to date it according to the years Stebbins was in Hudson — 1819–32. It is tempting to attribute this work to Francis W. Ed-munds, who was in the city of Hudson at least 1829–32, working as a cashier at the Hudson River Bank and painting in his spare time.

Although Edmunds' mother was a Quaker, his father and brother John W. (a lawyer of subsequent political im-portance) were active in the Hudson parish. Later Edmunds himself was ves-tryman in an Episcopal parish. Further ties between Edmunds and Stebbins are suggested by Edmund's notation in his European travel journal of a letter writ-ten to "C. Stebbins" in 1839. Some ele-ments of this portrait compare strongly to that done by Francis of his father, Samuel Edmunds.

Sherman and Lydia Deane Griswold (ca. 1837),
oil on canvas, 84" × 48", James E. Johnson.
Collections Columbia County Historical Society. Gift of
Mr. and Mrs. Charles Livingston Rundell in memory of
Mrs. Frank P. Rundell, Sr., great-granddaughter of
Sherman and Lydia Griswold, 1976.

Sherman Griswold (1790–1864) and his wife Lydia (1784–1845) were both descendants of early proprietors in the present towns of Austerlitz and Canaan, in the northeastern part of the county, where cloth manufacture spread and grew in the early years of the nineteenth century. This rendering dramatizes the importance of sheep to the community of this period. Handed down with the painting was a description of a custom that holds that the men of the Spencertown community would give salt to their sheep every Sunday after church. Around 1837, wool-growing and cloth manufacture were of principle importance to the county's economy. Besides the wool business, Sherman Griswold had invested in real estate; at one time he owned more than ten farms in the region. In 1837 a new business opportunity presented itself: the construction of a railway across Columbia County to the Berkshires offered great promise. Griswold sold most of his property, including the Hatfield Farm depicted in the painting, to raise funds for this investment. The Hudson and Berkshire railroad failed and all its enthusiastic investors lost their money.

James E. Johnson's large portrait of the Griswolds is one of the most interesting portraits in upstate New York. In it Johnson combines elements of romantic realism with a provincial iconography.

It is interesting to compare this nineteenth-century iconography with that of portraits from the first half of the eighteenth century. Most of the landscape backgrounds that appear in the earliest New York portraits are conventional and derived from European printed sources. Johnson painted identifiable landscapes relevant to the sitter.

James E. Johnson (1810–58) was born at Sandy Hill, Washington County, New York, and may be related to members of the Johnson family who moved to Spencertown in the early part of the nineteenth century. He is known to have painted in Sackett Harbor, New York, and in the Albany area in the 1830s. In 1846, he settled in Kinderhook as a permanent resident, and there, in 1853, married Sarah Ann Van Vleck. Numerous Johnson portraits of Spencertown and Kinderhook residents survive, suggesting the impact of this artist on a community.

Magdalena Van Hoesen Van Vleck (1828–68) was the sister-in-law of the artist's wife. Five more Van Vleck (or related) portraits by Johnson survive. Magdalena had married Peter H. Van Vleck, the enterprising journalist and printer who established the Kinderhook *Rough Notes* in 1854.

In portraits of young adults (such as Magdalena), adolescents, and children, Johnson exhibits a lightness and spontaneity appropriate to the age of his subjects. All his portraits suggest ability to convey close likenesses of his sitters.

New Concord House (1867), oil on canvas, 17¼" × 13¼", E. Morey. Courtesy Mr. and Mrs. James R. Piggot.

Magdalena Van Hoesen Van Vleck (1853), oil on canvas, 27½" × 22", James E. Johnson. Collection the Columbia County Historical Society. Gift of Mrs. Franklin J. Peterson, 1969.

Architectural paintings were a variant landscape theme that gave the artist an opportunity to portray the details of nature rather than the panoramic vista. The presence of human figures and man-made things, such as buildings and fences, create a comforting sense of the familiar that is lacking in traditional landscape paintings. Accurate details showing fence construction and open and closed shutters in use make such paintings excellent records. By the middle of the nineteenth century, photography tended to take over this function. Photography, however, did not have the capacity to take in the perspective of the road, house, and great tree in front of it.

130

Art students (ca. 1870). Claverack College and Hudson River Institute. Collections Columbia County Historical Society.

From the late eighteenth century onward, woman and girls took interest in the "ornamental" branches of education, which included instruction in various types of painting. Over a hundred-year period many types of subjects were painted; by the end of the nineteenth century, for example, amateur woman painters, such as those in this class taught by Laura Neely, were emulating the still life studies of academic painters.

Fruit in Glass Compote (1870–90), watercolor on paper with mica, 16" × 19½", Emma J. Cady. Courtesy Abby Aldrich Rockefeller Folk Art Collection

Two Birds on a Branch (1890), watercolor, pencil, and tempera on cardboard, 10" × 13⅞", Emma J. Cady. Courtesy Carl Black Art Research.

Many young women painted in watercolor, creating decorative pictures for their homes. Theorem paintings were popular, with stencils employed to make the outlines of the objects clear and crisp. Such paintings with similar compositions indicate identical design sources. Since the theorem painters made their own stencils, they had freedom to vary size and freehand details. Emma J. Cady's paintings are gracefully composed designs shaded with unusually delicate coloring. Her skillful use of stencils, mastery of watercolor technique, and treatment of textures (the shiny appearance of glass was

achieved by pasting tiny pieces of mica on the compote) have placed the works of this amateur high in American naive painting.

The fortuitous discovery of Two Birds on a Branch, inscribed on the reverse, "Mr. and Mrs. Eben N. Cady/Canaan/ Columbia County/N.Y./April 9, 1890/E. J. Cady/East Chatham/N.Y.", provides hitherto missing information about the residence and career of the creator of *Fruit in Glass Compote.*

Emma Jane Cady (1854–1933) lived with her parents, Norman and Mary E. Cady, near East Chatham, in a house closely resembling the home of Charlotte Temple Moore *(p. 93).* After the death of her parents (before 1912) she lived for a while with her brother Eben's son; by the early 1920s she was living in Michigan with her sister, and in Michigan she died. Historical materials compiled by the late Ray Lant of East Chatham and the recollections of his family indicate that she painted only in the earlier part of her life.

Gothic Revival

In the 1840s architect-designed buildings were both fashionable and popular. Until the end of the nineteenth century and well into the twentieth, people maintained an interest in the decorative effects of their homes and churches. Architects found the opportunity to earn their living by designing buildings, producing a rapid succession of styles derived from historical European sources. In these designs function and historical accuracy were subordinate to decorative elements.

Richard Upjohn of New York City was the leading architect in America working in the Gothic style in the 1840s and 1850s. His best known work, Trinity Church in New York City (1839), established his reputation and led to many commissions around the country, including three in Columbia County besides the remodeling of Martin Van Buren's home near Kinderhook. The popularity of the Gothic style, for which he is best known, led to the designs of other structures that survive in Columbia County, like the Gothic Cottage "Meadowbank" and two other churches. The taste for Gothic style continued until late in the century.

Meadowbank, the Norton Collin house (ca. 1840). Route 22, Hillsdale.

This description of Norton Collins home appeared in a column on "rural architecture and domestic economy" published in the Boston *Evening Transcript* in 1845:

MeadowBank Farm and Cottage Villa . . . my friend has placed his beautiful specimen of Rustic Gothic Architecture, on a meadow's bank, as the name implies, combining all the outlines of that most charming of all the orders, for domestic purposes. With its "gable" — "verge boards"—"bay windows"—"pinnacles"—"piazza" and "piazetts"—"its diamond cut glass doors" on front and rear—its "picturesque chimney-tops" yielding and receiving beauty; it is indeed a delightfully chosen as well as tastefully built residence, and the abode of a happy young couple, the lady herself having had an ample share in the outer as well as inner arrangements.

*Meadowbank tea service (1862), Ball, Black & Co.,
New York City.
Courtesy Miss Sybil H. May.*

On the twenty-fifth wedding anniversary of Norton and Eliza Park Collin, their daughters Eliza and Lucy presented their parents with this silver tea service. Lucy Collin designed the service depicting their parents' home.

Saint John the Evangelist Church (1846). Stockport.

The parish of Saint John the Evangelist was incorporated in 1845 by the owners and workers of the textiles mills in Stockport *(see p. 96)*. Joseph Marshall, a founder of the Hudson Print Works (the first cotton printing works in the state) was a church warden and, with two others, supervised the construction of this Gothic building. The architect is not known. On Christmas Eve 1847, a group of children of the mill owners took part in the first annual children's Christmas services. Miss Jane Stott daughter of Jonathan Stott, after whom neighboring Stottville was named, established this service as an occasion for giving gifts, a tradition that has been continued ever since at the "Little Brown Church."

133

Saint Paul's Episcopal Church (1852), designed by Richard Upjohn. Sylvester Street, Kinderhook.

In 1851 Richard Upjohn (1802–78) drew the plans for this church, which was built the next year on Chatham Street. In 1868 the building was moved to its present location on Sylvester Street.

A letter from Upjohn to Smith T. Van Buren of Kinderhook (in the collections of Columbia County Historical Society), one of the vestrymen of St. Paul's parish, indicates the changed roles of architect and builder. Talented builders like Barnabas Waterman or Benjamin Ambler, who interpreted copybook designs, were no longer entrusted with general plans.

We would observe in reference to furnishing general designs explain without working drawings that Mr. Upjohn has declined to make such for several years preferring [sic] at the same price to follow up with working drawings and see them properly executed.

A building erected from our general plans without working drawings made by us would be very likely to be quite a different affair from one made from the same plans with such working drawings — we have seen this practically demonstrated and the buildings as unlike as possible having any pretensions to have been made from the same plans.

The truth is it is as much as one can do to get mechanics & workmen to carry out our views with full size drawings before them and without such drawings it is out of the question they will not & cannot do it. We are aware that it takes us four times the trouble and labor but we also know that it is the only way to have anything properly done.

If good result could be produced from general plans we should have more good buildings as they would be taken from books — but an error in detail is frequently as fatal to good taste as bad outline — it is in the perfect harmony of the whole that we reach satisfaction. [written, NYC, Apr. 15, 1851]

Saint John's in the Wilderness Episcopal Church (1852), designed by Richard Upjohn. Copake.

The plans for St. John's in The Wilderness were prepared in 1851 by Upjohn and the building constructed the next year, with furnishings also designed by Upjohn. In the following year, he also made a set of plans for the parsonage, which was erected the same year.

This structure replaced the original Christ Church that was begun in the 1790s soon after Hudson was founded by New England immigrants. Church tradition had it that the second structure, begun in 1854, was based on the English style of Salisbury Cathedral. Only in their common Gothic inspiration are they similar, however. A tall steeple was destroyed in a storm some years ago.

Saint Luke's Episcopal Church (1859), designed by Richard Upjohn or Richard M. Upjohn. Route 9, Clermont.

The relatively elaborate detail on this small church suggests that Richard Upjohn's son, Richard M. Upjohn, had at least a hand in, if not total responsibility for, its design.

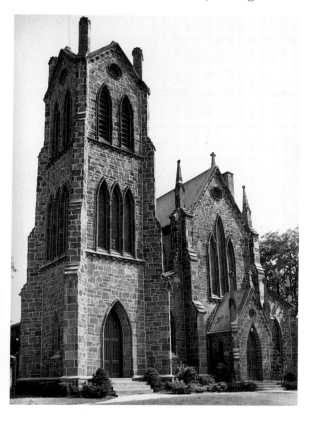

Christ Church (Episcopal) (1854–57), designed by William G. Harrison. Union and Court Streets, Hudson.

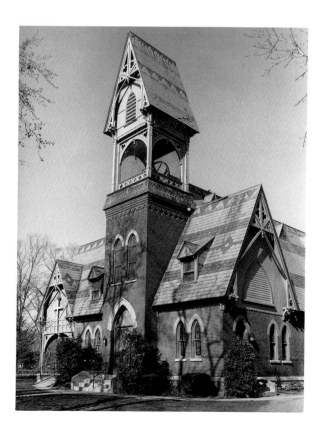

The Presbyterian Church (1877–78). Church Street, Valatie.

The Presbyterian Church of Valatie was organized in 1835, an outgrowth of the Second Reformed Church of Kinderhook founded two years before. The first structure of 1834 was superseded in 1878 by the completion of the present building, which was erroneously said to have been patterned after an "old German cathedral." It is a High Victorian Gothic structure of brick trimmed with blue limestone, the steep roofs covered with variegated slate. The exterior trim is painted green with red highlights. Interior furnishings are of natural finish spruce. Originally the church was lit by gas manufactured on the premises. An observer in 1878 described it "as one of the handsomest in the county."

Italianate Revival

Richard Upjohn's work was not restricted to Gothic designs. In fact, his first effort in Columbia County, Martin Van Buren's home, Lindenwald, was derived from Italian country villas of the Renaissance.

Although best known as the home of Martin Van Buren, Lindenwald began its interesting history as the Federal mansion constructed by General Peter Van Ness (1734–1804). He was born in what is now the township of Ghent; at the age of nineteen Van Ness commanded a company of soldiers in the British army that invaded French Canada in the French and Indian War (1754–63); in the Revolution he led a regiment in the Battle of Saratoga. Three years later in 1786 he purchased a tract of land of what was once Thomas Van Alstyne's farm *(p. 31)* near Kinderhook and lived in Thomas' stone house. He continued to be active in political circles as a member of the state convention that adopted the Constitution and served as a state senator, a member of the Council of Appointment, and the first judge of Columbia County court of common pleas. But before his cemetery marker recorded all these achievements, Peter Van Ness had made his most lasting mark. In 1797 he had built the house by which he is most readily remembered.

One of the earliest Federal structures in the county, Lindenwald (a name subsequently given to the property by Van Buren for its grove of Linden trees) was distinguished by its large and well-balanced proportions, subsequently much altered by Italianate additions in 1849. Much of the interior, however retains fine Federal woodwork.

Peter Van Ness' three sons were at least as distinguished as their father *(see p. 68)*. When his son William was living at Lindenwald, Washington Irving frequently visited as a guest and as tutor to William's children. It was during these visits that

Lindenwald, President Martin Van Buren National Historic Site, photograph of Richard Upjohn's rendering (1848). Route 9H, 2 miles south of Kinderhook. Collections of the Columbia County Historical Society

Irving acquired a knowledge of local history and personages that he later put to use in stories like "The Legend of Sleepy Hollow" *(see p. 33)*.

Lindenwald was sold from the family in 1834 and then in 1839, President Martin Van Buren, a native of Kinderhook, purchased the property as a future retirement home. He came to live at Lindenwald sooner than anticipated, as he was defeated for reelection in 1840. Van Buren then set about improving the house in the then-prevailing Italianate style. He commissioned Richard Upjohn, then doing other work in the county *(see p. 132)*, to design a wing on the rear, a bell tower, a front porch, dormers, and a central gable, bringing the house to a total of thirty-six rooms. Two unusual innovations by Van Buren were indoor "necessaries" and central heating. As a National Historic Site, Lindenwald is being preserved as a memorial to our eighth president, and its restoration will be to Van Buren's period as it appeared in Upjohn's 1848 sketch.

In 1843 John H. Reynolds (1819–75) married Margaret Whiting, the daughter of Colonel Charles Whiting, owner of the house, at that time consisting of only the rear portion. Reynolds began a law practice in Kinderhook and continued to work in the village until 1851, when he joined in partnership with John V. L. Pruyn of Albany. He apparently continued to reside in Kinderhook, at least during the summers, for in 1856 he build this large Italianate style house in the center of the village just in front of and attached to the early Dutch house that his father-in-law Gen. Charles Whiting had purchased and added to in 1853. After Reynolds' death the house became the property of Mrs. Sarah J. Bain, who added a porch; the next owner was her niece, Mrs. Mary Bain Reynolds, whose husband James Adger Reynolds was the son of John H. Reynolds, the builder of the house. This photograph was taken at about the time of their ownership.

The brick house is one of Columbia County's best

The John H. Reynolds house (ca. 1856), from a glass plate negative (ca. 1910), Kinderhook. Courtesy Rodney Gage.

examples of the Italian Villa. Based on an Italian vernacular, it also incorporates certain Renaissance forms. (Note the three-part Palladian windows and several dormers usually seen in earlier Georgian houses.) The asymmetrical arrangement of rooms around a tower (inspired by Italian bell towers), prominent brackets under the eaves, and a veranda or loggia, with round arches are all characteristic of this mid-nineteenth century revival, an attempt to recapture the picturesque romanticism of the Italian landscape paintings of the seventeenth and eighteenth centuries.

The early Dutch structure behind the main building was most likely to have been built by Jacobus Van Alen, who married in 1723. Before it was removed in the 1960s, it was described as having two rooms, each entered by a doorway nearly eight feet high. The windows were tall and narrow with leaded diamond-shaped panes giving an ecclesiastical appearance to the structure. The windows led one observer to suggest a relationship between this building and the early Dutch church (1717) that stood on adjacent property until 1813. It is likely that the leaded diamond panes were rare survivals, for no such relationship is borne out by land records. The house descended in the Van Alen family until at least 1795. It was built of brick, had heavy exposed beams and a steep roof line in keeping with other Dutch houses built before the mid-eighteenth century.

Brackets in the Italianate style, J. P. Chryster house (ca. 1856). Albany Avenue, Kinderhook.

Peaslee barn (ca. 1850s). Malden Bridge.

Horace W. Peaslee came from a farm family in New Lebanon. In his seventeenth year (1824) he apprenticed himself to become a millwright and soon became a machinist. He entered into partnership with Samuel Hanna in a foundry and machine shop at Valatie. In 1843 they purchased land at Malden Bridge and erected a substantial paper mill for the manufacture of wrapping paper and board. The mill prospered, and Peaslee built, nearby and overlooking his mill on the Kinderhook Creek, a substantial house. Adjacent to the house, he built a most unusual carriage barn in conjunction with the large farm he operated. The barn is in the Italianate style, an unusual elegance for such a utilitarian structure. It is all the more unusual because it is capped by not one but two cupolas arising from a roof that slants in several directions.

Functional outbuildings retained their basic shapes, but application of Gothic and Italianate ornaments greatly altered their appearance.

Gazebo, Crow Hill. Route 9H, Kinderhook.

Privy in Italianate style , Claverack.

Garden shed, Henry Van Schaack house. Stuyvesant.

The banneret form of this vane is based on early weathervane design adopted from the small flags or pennants that once flew from castles in Europe and Great Britain. While the overall design is like that of the First Presbyterian Church (Hudson) vane *(page 108)*, the construction of this vane, the manner in which the arrow has been incorporated into the design, and the elaborate scrolled outline are marks of later construction.

Later nineteenth-century rural churches in Columbia County were often built in the traditional form of eighteenth-century New England meeting houses *(pages 90 and 95)*, in which weathervanes were a prominent part of their design, a practice that was followed in later churches. Although the cock and fish, religious and rural symbols, were popular motifs in the seventeenth and eighteenth centuries, most of the vanes that survive do not carry any particular religious significance.

Farm animals were often used as motifs for rural vanes. In the late nineteenth century, weathervanes were used more often on barns and other outbuildings than on houses. By that time, they were often adapted for use as lightning rods grounded to wire cables. Fashionable houses used either plain or wrought iron rods or ornaments to protect the building from lightning.

Wind indicators aided farmers in weather forecasting. The weather itself, along with signs of the seasons, were an important part of the planting and harvesting cycles yearly observed by farmers.

Often the gable end of a building would be adorned with a vane; simple buildings, like barns and smokehouses *(page 58)*, gained some visual interest as a result.

Weathervane, Hillsdale Methodist Episcopal Church (erected 1845), Hillsdale.

Weathervane, Martindale Community Gospel Church, Martindale.

Weathervane, nineteenth-century barn. Livingston.

Weathervane, nineteenth-century barn. Stuyvesant.

Weathervane, barn. Canaan.

The design of this vane bears a striking similarity to others manufactured in the later decades of the nineteenth century and illustrated in manufacturers' catalogues, although the incorporation of a date into the design is unusual. The form is a representation of the banneret — in this instance, a flag.

(Below) Simons General Store (1874), built by Martin Luther Hills. Ancram.

This general store has been in continuous operation ever since it first opened. Its present name derives from Edward T. Simons, who owned it from 1924 to 1971. Recently it was restored to its late-nineteenth-century appearance with most of its early furnishings intact. It is the commercial focal point of the village of Ancram.

Ancram, named for Robert Livingston's Scottish birthplace, got its start as a community when Philip Livingston established iron works here in 1748. For many years these were the only iron works in New York. In the nineteenth century the mining and reduction of iron ore was a major industry in this part of Columbia County, in the neighboring areas of Dutchess County, and in Massachusetts and Connecticut. This industry led to Ancram's becoming a railroad junction, which, combined with a modest number of other industries, gave the community reasonable prosperity through the nineteenth century. Today its surviving industry is a paper mill on the site of the original Livingston iron furnace.

The general store is a remarkably well-preserved example of the Italianate style including a cupola and an elaborate two-story piazza as its key visual element.

At first stylistic architecture was limited to people of means. Later in the nineteenth century, it was widely adapted for all kinds of buildings. Mechanization of cutting tools greatly aided in the manufacture of the intricately designed ornaments used on such buildings.

Charles Housman was a Manhattan real estate broker who built two residences in Columbia County. One, in Valatie, was an impressive Second Empire house with elaborate gardens and a conservatory. His summer place at New Concord was an old house that he elaborately remodeled and added to; part of it still stands. He had built for his two small daughters this small, charming playhouse, which is stylistically related to the nineteenth-century revival styles. For example, in the 1850s architects were influenced by the so-called Swiss architecture, where interior beams were repeated on the exterior for functional and decorative effect. An elaborate example of this use is to be seen on the Valatie Presbyterian Church *(p. 135);* here a small-scale adaptation of the style is the gable over the entrance.

The playhouse was moved from New Concord to Spencertown in 1946 and to a second location in Spencertown in 1953. Appropriately the house has been used as a private doll museum.

Playhouse (1875). South Street, Spencertown.

The Elbert Michael house (1888). Mellenville, Claverack.

Elbert Michael was born in 1855 on the family homestead in Martindale, a son of Anthony and Charlotte Michael. He owned and worked two farms in Taconic and in Snydertown. In 1875 he married Emma Jean Concklin, and they had two children. In 1888 he built this home in Mellenville and resided in the hamlet until he died, when the house was inherited by his son, Dr. Reynard Michael, D.D.S.

Even grand styles like the Second Empire with its mansard roof and bracketed cornices can be successfully adapted to small houses. This little house is a case in point. It is also a good example of good maintenance and careful preservation. For example, when a fireplace was incorporated into the house in recent years, the existing bay window and dormer were used to accommodate the chimney by enclosing the window openings with compatible paneling. The result is a perfect illusion — that which is changed is unrecognizable as anything but original.

Samuel J. Tilden II house (1894). Routes 20 and 22, Lebanon.

Samuel J. Tilden was the nephew and namesake of the former New York governor who nearly became president *(see p. 155)*. As a young man he was an executive in the family business, Tilden Pharmaceutical Co. of Lebanon. In 1890 he married Augusta Halsey of Brooklyn, an energetic planner who set out to select a site for a dream house in Lebanon. To her husband's undoubted embarrassment, she selected the site that the Mount Lebanon Shakers owned and used to cultivate herbs for their medicinal factory — one that was sometimes in competition with the Tilden firm. Through a third party, however, a sale was completed for a twenty-acre plot. The Tilden's retained an architect; but apparently Mrs. Tilden did much of the planning for their twenty-five room home, including the design of paneled wood ceilings, convex French plate glass windows; stained glass windows, and carved marble mantels.

The style of the house is basically "Queen Anne," which has less to do with that English monarch than with country estates designed by Richard W. Show in the 1860s and 1870s in England, a style that vaguely recalled rural country houses of the medieval style before Queen Anne's time. In America the style became popular in the 1880s and 1890s. It was interpreted in our natural idiom of wood, often in shingles, earning it the name of "shingle style." These houses developed into a highly eloquent vernacular — an organic character that expresses the purpose and nature of the structure: wings, towers, porches, and other appendages created a complex pile on the outside, but a functionally rationalized arrangement of rooms on the inside. The use of central heating, for example, enabled interiors to be opened up to provide a new sense of space. The versatility of shingled walls permitted irregular wall shapes including curved and flanged walls, which fitted nicely into the era's concern for functional design and appreciation of natural materials. These innovations are aptly expressed in the Samuel J. Tilden II house, probably Columbia County's best example of this type of architecture.

142

After the Civil War two developments resulted in important changes in architecture. One was a design philosophy that maintained that the usefulness and purpose of a building was its most important feature. This admiration of nature was a philosophy borrowed from romanticism, as natural materials or natural environment were used to create a functional form in which stylistic elements played a subordinate role. The other development was technological: by the middle of the nineteenth century prefabricated structural components could be cast in iron. The Civil War interrupted its manufacture, but after the war iron components that could be cast into any type of ornamental shape were manufactured and used to replace traditional wood and masonry.

Union Station (1887),
designed by Shepley, Rutan, and Coolidge. Chatham.
From a postcard (ca. 1900).
Courtesy the Chatham Courier.

The village of Chatham, although begun in 1812, only began to prosper when it became a railroad junction between Albany and Boston and later (1869) to points north and south. A century ago more than one hundred trains passed through Chatham each day. In the center of the village, the Boston and Albany Railroad had a station built in 1886–87 by the firm of Shepley, Rutan, and Coolidge, disciples of Henry H. Richardson, America's leading architect at that time. Richardson had designed nine stations for the Boston and Albany Railroad between 1881 and 1886; and when he died in the latter year, the three men formed a successor firm under their own names, and continued for some time to design in the manner of their mentor. The Chatham station closely resembles two done by Richardson at Auburndale and Holyoke, Massachusetts.

Richardson's design philosophy is reflected in the new firm's train station at Chatham. He had maintained that a station's function was that of a temporary shelter and that the design of the structure must, above all, reflect its use. Prior to Richardson, architectural design tended to place primary emphasis on decorative effect. In keeping with its role as a temporary shelter, the Chatham station has long expanses of protective roofs, with only secondary emphasis on the stylistic appearance of the facade. Union Station, as a fine example of this important change in America's orientation to architecture, has been placed on the National Register of Historic Places.

Covered bridges. Hudson Street, County Route 21, Kinderhook.

Stone arch bridge. Route 9J, Stuyvesant.

This may be the oldest surviving bridge in Columbia County. Built when this river road was but one lane wide, it has survived decades of neglect since being bypassed by an enlarged Route 9J (in background). Unaltered by a century or more of floods, freezing, and growing tree roots, this simple stone arch may outlast all other bridges in Columbia County.

These large (double lane) covered bridges spanned the Kinderhook Creek at the southeast entrance to the village of Kinderhook up until 1929 when they were removed. Covered bridges were first mentioned in the first decades of the nineteenth century and were built throughout most of that century. Numerous bridge designers patented their own truss designs. The truss bridges at Kinderhook were built on the Town lattice-truss design, patented by Ithiel Town of Connecticut in 1820. For rights to use his patent, builders of this type of bridge paid royalties of one dollar per foot. Many Town lattice-truss bridges were built throughout the county, testifying not only to its unusual strength but to Town's excellent salesmanship.

There were several practical reasons for covering a bridge: to preserve the timbers from wet weather; to keep the roadway dry; to strengthen the bridge structure; and to keep the timbers from drying out and becoming loose at the joints.

Whipple truss bridge (1870). Van Wyck Lane, Claverack.

This double-span iron bridge was built from a design patented in 1841 by Squire Whipple of Utica and Albany, who is recognized by civil engineers as the father of American bridge building because of this patented iron bridge that became the standard for much of early metal truss bridge technology. The cast and wrought iron "arch truss" (This one has a segmental bowstring truss) was the first type of iron bridge extensively used for highways in America.

J. D. Hutchinson of Troy built this eighty-one foot two-span bridge over the Claverack Creek in 1870. It is the only known surviving multiple-span example of its type.

The Spangler Bridge (1880). Spangler Road, Chatham.

The Spangler Bridge was erected over the Kinderhook Creek in 1880 to give farmers on the east side of the creek access to a large gristmill (still extant) on the west side. Undisturbed by through traffic, the bridge remains essentially unchanged since the time of its erection. It is one of only a few remaining bridges built by the Morse Bridge Company of Youngstown, Ohio, and the only one surviving in New York State. This 138-foot bridge is of the "high Pratt truss" type consisting of two Pratt trusses, each truss composed of an upper chord, a lower chord, and seven posts creating eight panels. Each panel contains diagonal and counterbracing that forms an X in each panel. Unusually fanciful cast iron brackets create an arch at either entrance, and four cast iron urns formerly crowned the portal bracing.

The neighboring mill for which the bridge is named was owned by a man named Spengler. The date at which the spelling shifted is unknown.

Octagon house, built for Dr. John D. Reynolds (ca. 1866–68). Copake.

Today there are less than a hundred octagon houses in New York State, three of which are in Columbia County. The once fashionable, faddish form was inspired by Orson Squire Fowler's book, *A Home for All,* published in 1848 and 1853. As a designer Fowler anticipated the twentieth-century philosophy of form following function. He espoused the superior aesthetics of a circular object as opposed to a rectangular one, pointing out that the octagon form had one-fifth less wall space than the same amount of floor space in a rectangular house, and therefore provided greater heating efficiency. In this type of house ample windows on eight sides offered the advantages of continual sunshine and good cross ventilation, Fowler's designs made use of conventional building materials and traditional decorations.

After his return from the Civil War, Dr. John Reynolds built this octagon house at Copake Flats. Departing from the traditional octagon plan, he added a wing for his office. The porch was originally open and the roof was of wood shingles. Once an octagonal window existed in a bedroom, but it has since been closed up. The cobblestone chimney and foundation facing is unusual for an octagon house; they may reflect the personal interest of some past owner who also installed an unusual rock garden in the yard: each rock is in the shape of an animal.

Each side of the octagon is twelve feet long, creating a distance from side to side of 28 feet. Originally the rooms and woodwork were painted white, the color recommended by Fowler.

Other octagon houses in Columbia County are located at Ancramdale and Columbiaville. Often mistaken for a fourth octagon is the hexagonal house near the Columbiaville one (Route 9).

Ezra Waterbury house (ca. 1869). 124 Warren Street, Hudson.

"The only cast iron front building built exclusively as a residence" is how this house is described by today's Friends of Cast-Iron Architecture, the leading organization for the study and preservation of this type of architecture, unique to America.

In architecture perhaps nothing expresses the arrival of the Industrial Revolution in America better than the innovation of the prefabricated cast iron front building. This important innovation in nineteenth-century architecture got its start in New York City (which still has more cast iron buildings than any other) through the efforts of inventor James Bogardus who built the first all-iron building in America in 1849 and many more thereafter. Bogardus, born in Catskill, New York just across the Hudson River from Columbia County, began a profound change in commercial architecture that continued for half a century and presaged the glass curtain and steel skyscrapers of today.

Foundries cast modular parts that, when bolted together and attached to the front of a structure, formed elaborate facades in imitation of costly stone work. It was quicker to make, more elaborate, cheaper, and stronger than the stone buildings it imitated. It permitted large expanses of window glass, and it has proved to be more durable than stone. Most cast iron facades are done in the form of columns, porticoes, and balconies; but only a very few survive with the Waterbury house's smooth effect of ashlar, in imitation of an unbroken facade of flat-faced stone blocks. Two similar structures built about 1869 on Grand Street in New York City bear the foundry label of J. L. Jackson & Brothers, a firm that held a patent for this design for iron fronts in imitation of ashlar. Jackson may have produced the iron for the Waterbury house.

Ezra Waterbury was born in 1821 in Lebanon. He lived there after his marriage in 1842 until about 1868, when he came to Hudson and joined Benjamin R. Millard in the brewery business. He later had different partners and produced an ale called "Present Use." He owned several properties in Hudson; and in January 1869, purchased from Abram Bogardus and Sherman Van Ness the property at 124 Warren Street. Van Ness and Bogardus were in business together in that year as suppliers of coal, wood, and building materials at 65 Diamond Street; and they both resided on Warren Street in Hudson. In 1886 Waterbury sold the house to Michael McArdle, another Hudson business man, for $7500.

Landscape Painters

The last half of the nineteenth century saw Columbia County's best artists, those who were most academically accomplished. First among them was Frederick E. Church, who had been so impressed by a view from a hill south of Hudson that he bought the hill and there erected his great house, Olana. Other landscape painters came to Columbia County, but of most interest are the several who were native and painted local scenes as well as traveling to other places. Sanford Gifford, the Parton brothers, John Bristol, and Henry Loop were accomplished contemporaries. This generation of artists brought American art its first international prominence. Painters were elevated to the status of "artist." Superior training by art academies (principally in New York City), exploration of Europe's art heritage, and the fact that photography had freed the artist from his responsibility of strict recorder — all contributed to a self-conscious, "art-for-art's-sake" role for these painters. This, combined with the romantic era's celebration of the beauty of American nature, brought the landscapes of the Hudson River school to the highest prominence, and Columbia County had a real part in it.

Olana, The Frederick Edwin Church home (1870–74; 1888–90). Route 9G, Greenport. Olana State Historic Site.

There is a high hill south of the city of Hudson that commands an unparalleled view of the upper Hudson River valley and the Catskill Mountains beyond. To this hill Frederick Church (1826–1900) brought his bride in 1860. A decade later, with the help of architect Calvert Vaux, Church and his wife began to build their dream house on the very top of this hill, which they called Olana, ("our place on high"). Drawing on his travels in the Middle East, Church created a thirty-seven room personal expression in a Persian style. The house was completed in 1874 and then enlarged (1888–90) by a studio wing on the west side, overlooking the river that gave its name to America's first internationally recognized school of art, the Hudson River school in which Church was a leader.

Olana remained in the Church family until the late 1960s, when it was acquired by the New York State Historic Trust. It is now a historic site open to the public.

Winter Scene, Olana (ca. 1870), oil on canvas, 20" × 18", Frederick E. Church. Olana State Historic Site, New York State Office of Parks and Recreation.

This view of the Hudson River and the south grounds of Olana was done by Church about the time he began his large house on this site. It is a field study, a small rough oil sketch done outdoors to be used later in the studio as a reference for a final painting. Despite the unpolished effect of the sketch, this painting still has a facility and power that mark Church's work and that established him as the leading American landscapist by the 1850s.

Church was brought up in Hartford, Connecticut, by his father, a prosperous insurance man who supported his son's desire to study art. Church studied with, among others, Thomas Cole of Catskill, the founder of the American landscape school. Church went on to become Cole's successor, painting major landscapes of the places he visited in South America, Europe, and the Middle East as well as in America. His heart seems to have remained in the Hudson valley, for in 1860 he returned with his young wife to the hill they called Olana, across the river from where his mentor, Thomas Cole, had had his studio.

View from Church Hill, Olana (1846), oil on canvas, Arthur Parton. Courtesy Olana State Historic Site, New York State Office of Parks and Recreation.

Arthur Parton (1842–1914), born in Hudson, New York, was the eldest of three brothers (Ernest and Henry were the other two) who became well-known artists in the nineteenth century. Arthur was a member of the National Academy and exhibited widely, often winning prizes for his landscapes. He was a friend of Frederick E. Church, and it was from Church's property that he painted this view, before Church undertook extensive landscaping there. The view is essentially the same as the one Church did himself in 1870 (*p. 149*).

This painting by Parton is an example of his early period, when he worked under the influence of Church and others who strove to paint with the highest fidelity to nature. By the 1880s, however, American taste had changed toward the looser brushwork and somber colors of the new, almost impressionistic landscape painting. Unlike Church and Gifford, Arthur Parton changed his style, and with others carried the Hudson River school into its third and last "generation" — taking the movement up to the end of the nineteenth century.

Sanford Gifford (1823–80) was born in Saratoga County. Within the year the family moved to Hudson where his father established an iron foundry. Sanford withdrew from college in his first year to embark on a career as an artist. He first attempted portraiture but gave it up in favor of landscape painting. He was much influenced by Thomas Cole and, without formal training, succeeded in being exhibited at the National Academy of Design at the age of twenty-four. By his thirty-first year he was a full member of the Academy. From then on he traveled widely in Europe and America, keeping a sketch book of subjects for future paintings. This painting shows great sensitivity, especially in its study of light and atmosphere. The brushwork is exact, the strokes nearly invisible; his subjects realistic yet subordinate to his primary interest — the effects of light on land and water. This view of South Bay and Mount Merino, one of many he painted of that scene, was owned by Robert Gordon in 1881, and was number 378 in the *Memorial Catâlogue* of Gifford's works published that year.

South Bay, on the Hudson, near Hudson, N.Y. (1864), 12¼" × 25¼", Sanford R. Gifford.
Courtesy of Sotheby Parke Bernet, Inc., New York.

Landscape (ca. 1860), oil on canvas, 30½" × 50¼",
John Bunyan Bristol. Columbia County Historical Society.
Gift of Thomas A. Larramore, 1960.

John Bristol (1826–1909) was born in Hillsdale and was a virtually self-taught painter of the Hudson River school, though he had a few lessons from Henry Ary of Hudson *(see p. 126)*. He was elected an Associate of the National Academy in 1859 and an academician in 1875. From 1860 on, he lived in New York City but spent his summers in Great Barrington and on tours in neighboring states. His paintings are landscapes of these areas. The one illustrated here is not identified as to location but is characteristic of his style. The figure in the foreground is presumably the artist himself.

J. B. Bristol (1860), oil on canvas, Henry Loop, National Academy of Design. Frick Art Reference Library.

Bristol (1826–1909) and Loop (1831–1895) both grew up in Hillsdale. When Bristol was elected an associate of the National Academy in 1859, he was required to present his portrait within one year. This painting is the result. Henry Augustus Loop became a portrait and figure painter, studying first with Henry Peters Gray in New York City and then in various places in Europe. He was himself elected an associate of the National Academy in 1861. Four years later he married his most talented student, Jennette Harrison, who also became an associate of the Academy. One of their daughters became a portrait painter as well. Like Bristol and many other artists of their day, Loop exhibited in the Centennial Exposition of 1876. Except for a tour of Europe, he spent most of his life working in his New York City studio, with excursions to Columbia County and other Hudson valley localities. Among his many portraits are ones of Worthington Wittridge and Russell Sage.

Cows at Pasture (1899), oil on canvas,
16" × 20¼", Cortland C. Van Deusen.
Columbia County Historical Society.
Gift of Miss Elizabeth Sutherland, 1940.

Van Deusen (1853–1913) was born in Hudson, the son of a shoemaker and the eighth generation of his family in the county. He attended Claverack Academy and Rutgers University and read law in Columbia County. According to family tradition, his art avocation began as a student of an otherwise unidentified Mr. Prior of Hudson. He is also said to have traveled from his home in Canaan to Hudson to take lessons. George McKinstry, among others, was giving art lessons there at that time (1870–80). One of his friends, years later, recalled that Van Deusen preferred to paint landscapes and oil compositions in the field. He also copied some portraits. About fifty paintings by him are known; many like the one illustrated here are of pastoral scenes realistically rendered in the manner of the second generation of the Hudson River school, but made at the time (1890s) when any artist of that school who expected to make a living at painting was doing sketchy, light-filled canvases of the impressionistic mode. Van Deusen was sustained by his law practice and seems to have painted for his own enjoyment.

In November 1876 a son of Columbia County was for the second time elected President of the United States. The victory was bittersweet, for votes in the Electoral College were maneuvered away from him, and Samuel Tilden never took the office for which he had received a popular mandate.

Grave of Samuel Tilden. Cemetery of the Evergreens, Lebanon.

Born in Lebanon (1814), a successful New York City lawyer, political ally of Martin Van Buren, governor of the State of New York, President-elect of the United States (elected by popular vote but not by the Electoral College), and a founder of the New York Public Library, Samuel Tilden chose to be buried in Lebanon on a grassy knoll in the center of the Evergreens (1886). His impressive monument stands apart from all others, surrounded by a wide circle of granite curbing, as if in acknowledgement of his important career.

While his younger brother, Henry, established the earliest of the large pharmaceutical companies in America in his hometown of Lebanon, Samuel Tilden pursued a legal career in New York City. He allied himself with a good friend of his father's, fellow county resident and Democrat, Martin Van Buren, an alliance that led to his running for state attorney general in 1855. Although he lost, in part due to a split in the party the year before, he remained active in the newly reshaped Democratic Party. After the Civil War his party favored policies of sound money, honest government, and support for the working man. But in his own state the corrupt Tweed ring controled the party. Tilden, however, gained the chairmanship of the Democratic Committee and was able to expose and depose the Tweed faction. As a result he was elected governor in 1874. In this office he gained a nationwide reputation as reformer with his nonpartisan investigation of the canal frauds. When he ran for President in 1876, he won a majority of the popular votes, but lost the office in the Electoral College when some delegates did not follow their states' directive. This disillusioning experience prompted his reassertion of the view that the power of government was vested in the people but that the people must act; thus his epitaph: "I still trust the people."

In private life he distinguished himself as one of the three founders of the New York Public Library, contributing his own extensive library and an endowment to help establish one of the great library systems in the country.

Columbia County Courthouse (1900), Hudson.

By the latter part of the nineteenth century the law had grown in its sophistication and politics in its corruption. Yet the fourth courthouse of Columbia County was topped by a figure of justice in a traditional design.

This, the fourth courthouse, was built in 1900. Its style was traditional classic revival style common to public buildings in America from the late eighteenth century up to the 1930s, despite the fact that in residential building it was considered passé by the 1840s.

By the end of the century, Hudson had a resident architect — a true architect, not a designer-contractor, as had been customary since the eighteenth century, but a person who exclusively made architectural designs to be executed by contractors. This person was Henry S. Moul (b. 1857). Although a descendant of Ghent settlers, he was born outside the county and came to Hudson in 1875. He served an apprenticeship in carpentry with James E. McClure and studied architecture in his spare time. By 1880 he took over his employer's business and then in 1896 dispensed with contracting and dedicated his business solely to architectural design. Besides the courthouse he designed several fine Hudson houses. He was also an active parishioner of the Methodist Episcopal Church and a supervisor for Hudson Third Ward. Through his civic service and his buildings, he made a significant contribution to the city of Hudson.

The following is a checklist of painters related to Columbia County. The list has been compiled from nineteenth-century exhibition records, newspapers, county directories, genealogical publications, and twentieth-century commentary, catalogues, and records. The list is full, but not intended to be complete. Its purpose is to indicate the scope of painting in the county. Unless otherwise noted, the painters here are known only to have visited the county. Page references are provided for those who are represented in this book.

Albrecht, Silas W. (n. d.), landscape painter; Germantown, ca. 1880–90.

*Ames, Ezra (1768–1836), active in Albany 1793–1836. (p. 71)

†Ary, Henry (1807–59), landscape and portrait painter, instructor; Hudson, ca. 1840–59. (p. 127)

Baker, C[harles?] (1839–ca. 1888), landscape painter at Greenport. (p. 118)

Beers, Martha Stuart (n. d.), still-life painter; New Lebanon; ca. 1830.

Bidwell, Mary W. (n. d.), landscape painter; Copake, ca. 1867.

Billingham, John R. (n. d.), listed in Hudson directories 1881–1910; work unknown.

Brandard, R. (n. d.), engraver; view of Hudson, ca. 1840.

Brevoort, James Renwick (1832–1918), landscape painter; exhibited painting of "Chatham, N. Y." in 1847; other views listed were of Chatham, New Jersey.

‡Bristol, Edward (n. d.); landscape painter; exhibited at Brooklyn Art Association in 1868. Possibly a brother of John Bristol.

‡Bristol, John B. (1826–1909), landscape painter, born in Hillsdale. (p. 152)

Browere, Albertus D. O. (1814–1887), landscape and genre painter; lived at Catskill, associated with Hudson artists during the 1840s and 1850s. (p. 125)

Brownell, Charles De Wolfe (1822–1909), landscape painter; landscape sketch of Olana, 1886.

Bunner, Andrew Fisher (1841–97), landscape painter; Claverack, 1866.

‡Cady, Emma Jane (1854–1933), amateur painter, active ca. 1870–95, at East Chatham. (p. 131)

Case, Edith (n. d.), landscape painter; Ghent, 1895.

* Portrayed eminent county citizens but lived or worked outside the county.
† Lived in the county.
‡ Born in the county.

Chubb, Frederick Y. (ca. 1838–n. d.), landscape painter; Claverack Creek, 1866 (see Bunner).

Church, Frederic E. (1826–1900), landscape painter; resident from 1860s through 1900. (p. 149)

Coates, [E. C.?], landscape painter; exhibited "Landscape View on Hudson," 1841.

‡Collins, Lucy (n. d.), portrait and landscape painter; Hillsdale, active 1860s–80s. (p. 133)

Cranch, C. R. (1813–92), landscape painter; Columbia County view, 1852.

Cromwell, D. H. (n. d.), portraits, profiles; worked with physiognotrace; advertised in Hudson in 1808.

Currier and Ives, lithographers, New York City; "Shakers at New Lebanon"; active 1857–1907.

de Forest, Lockwood (1850–n. d.), landscape painter; Columbia County view, 1873.

de Haas, Mauritz Frederick Hendrik (1832–95), born in Rotterdam, Netherlands; instructor at Claverack College and Hudson River Institute; after 1859 in New York City; noted as marine painter; Civil War scenes.

Dixey, John V. (n. d.), landscape painter; active 1827–41; "View near Hudson," 1833.

Dunnel, John Henry (1813–1904), landscape painter; "Marino Point, near Hudson," 1848.

Durand, A. B. (1796–1886), landscape painter; in Hillsdale 1861; exhibited views in Hillsdale area. (p. 119)

Duyckinck, Gerardus (1695–ca. 1746), portrait painter; active in New York City, ca. 1717–46; in Columbia County during 1730s and 1740s. (p. 37)

Duyckinck, Gerardus (1723–97), limner, instructor, dealer in art supplies at New York City and Albany County; in Columbia County 1779.

‡Edmunds, Francis William (1806–63), genre painter, occasional portrait painter; active in Hudson in 1820s and 1830s. (p. 128)

Ferguson, Henry Augustus (1832–1911), landscape painter; Columbia County view 1898–99.

Field, Erastus Salisbury (1805–1900), portrait and history painter; active in Hudson, 1828–early 1830s. (p. 120)

Flaherty, J. T. (n. d.), active in Philadelphia; copied Claverack church view, 1883.

†Freeborn, Sara (n. d.–1906), landscape painter and sculptress, living in Hudson from youth through 1876.

Frost, A. B. (n. d.), noted art student at Claverack College and Hudson River Institute.

Fulton, Robert (1765–1815), turned from art to engineering; county resident 1806–15.

‡Fulton, Harriet Livingston (1786–1824), miniaturist; sketches; wife of Robert Fulton.

Gay, Edward (1837–1928), landscape painter; Columbia County view 1867.

†Gifford, Sanford Robinson (1823–80), landscape painter; living in Hudson from 1824; buried at Hudson; painted landscapes from 1846; traveled in American and Europe. (p. 151)

Goodell, I. C. (1800–ca. 1875), portrait painter; active in Columbia County ca. 1832–34. (p. 123)

Graner, Grace (n d.), listed in Hudson directories 1894–95.

Harding, John L. (n. d.), portrait painter, active at Albany 1835–38; in Columbia County 1835.

Harny, James (probably James M. Hart, 1828–1901), exhibited "Claverack Creek," 1846, Pennsylvania Academy of Fine Arts.

‡Hatch, Elisha (n. d.), amateur portrait painter; Canaan, New York, ca. 1830–40.

Heinrich, F. H. (n. d.), active in New York City, 1848–ca. 1852; exhibited Columbia County scene, 1852.

Hillyer, William (n. d.), portrait painter, active in New York 1832–64; worked in Kinderhook in 1832.

†Hoyle, Raphael (1804–38), landscape painter; born in England; painted Hudson Valley scenes; resided at Hudson in 1836.

Inman, Henry (1801–46), landscape, portrait, and genre painter; "Claverack Falls," 1844; portrait of Martin Van Buren.

*Jarvis, John Wesley (1780–1840), portrait painter; portrait of Mordecai Myers, officer, War of 1812.

†Johnson, James E. (ca. 1810–58), born Washington County, portrait painter, active Columbia County ca. 1837–58. (p. 129)

Juman, H. (n. d.), landscape painter, sketch of "Claverack Falls, Columbia County, New York," 1831.

Kensett, John (1816–72), landscape painter; views of Bash Bish Falls taken from Columbia County.

†Kittell, Nicholas Biddle (1822–94), portrait painter; probably born at Kinderhook; parents married there 1820.

Lanman, Charles (1819–95), landscape painter (and writer); friend of F. W. Edmunds; painted Bash Bish Falls, 1888.

Lazarus, A. J. (n. d.), portrait painter; portrait of Dr. George Livingston.

LeClear, Thomas (1818–82), portrait painter; portraits of Hudson and Kinderhook residents known.

Lasher, Sally (n. d.), amateur painter; view of docks at Germantown, ca. 1875. Likely to be native resident.

‡Livingston, Henry (n. d.), landscape painter, Hudson and Mohawk Valley scenes, active 1790s.

‡Livingston, Montgomery (1816–n. d.), landscape painter; active 1838–52. Son of Chancellor Robert L. Livingston.

‡Livingston, Dr. Edward (n. d.), landscape painter; active 1839–early 1840s.

‡Loop, Henry A. (1831–95), portrait figure painter; born in Hillsdale. (p. 153)

Loop, Jennette S. H. (1840–1909), portrait painter, wife of Henry A. Loop.

Lossing, Benson J. (1813–91), landscape painter, engraver and illustrator, Columbia County scenes, 1860.

Lodet, P. (n. d.), landscape watercolor painter; visited county in 1806. (p. 62 and 75)

‡Ludlow, Robert Fulton (n. d.), landscape and portrait painter; listed in Hudson directories 1894–95; lived in Claverack. (p. 62 and 75)

Martin, Homer (1837–97), landscape painter, Bash Bish Falls, 1859.

McIlworth, Thomas (n. d.), active in New York 1757–67; portrait painter; portrait of Margaret Beekman Livingston. (p. 47)

‡McKinstry, George A. (1855–1919), landscape and portrait painter; born at Hudson.

‡Meluis, Howard (n. d.), landscape painter; listed in county business directories, 1871–81.

‡Miller, Louisa F. (n. d.) amateur painter; New Lebanon, ca. 1830.

‡Morey, E[dward?] (n. d.), landscape painter, New Concord, 1867. (p. 130)

Palmer, Walter Launt (1854–n. d.), landscape painter; studied with Church at Hudson, 1870–72.

‡Parton, Arthur (1842–1914), landscape and still-life painter, born in Hudson. (p. 150)

‡Parton, Ernest (1845–1919), landscape painter; born in Hudson; buried in Hudson cemetery.

‡Parton, Henry W. (1858–1933), landscape, still-life, and portrait painter; born in Hudson; buried in Hudson cemetery.

‡Parton, Hulda (n. d.), portrait and still-life painter; daughter of Arthur Parton, born in Hudson.

Neely, Laura (n. d.), instructor at Claverack College and Hudson River Institute.

Phillips, Ammi (1788–1865), portrait painter; worked in Columbia County at intervals between 1814 and 1834. (p. 69 and 120–21)

‡Phillips, Bert G. (1865–1956), Indian and mural painter; born in Hudson.

Prime, H. F. (ca. 1811–1841), portrait painter; worked at Hudson, late 1830s–41. (p. 124)

Reisner, Martin A. (n. d.), landscape painter; "Scene near Canaan, New York," 1859.

†Richards, Thomas Addison (1820–1900), landscape painter; said to have resided briefly at Hudson; painted Columbia County area ca. 1845–57.

Robertson, Archibald (1765–1835) or Alexander (1772–1841), brothers of Scottish birth who emigrated to America in the early 1790s; one of them sketched "Clermont, Seat of Mrs. Livinston," and signed it "A. Robertson" in 1796. (p. 49)

Sidney, Wilbur (n. d.), landscape painter; watercolor of Hudson, 1824.

Sonntag, William Louis (1822–1900), landscape painter; Columbia County, 1854.

‡Stark, George (n. d.), history painter; came from Spencertown to Claverack College and Hudson River Institute.

†Stever, Josephine (n. d.), amateur painter; active at Philmont ca. 1890–1910.

*Stuart, Gilbert (1755–1828), portrait painter; studied in England; active at Philadelphia and Boston. (p. 60 and 68)

Sutcliff, Robert (n. d.), born in England; sketched "Sunnyside," the Claverack home of his cousin, active 1805.

Talbot, Jesse (1806–79), landscape painter; "Port Merino on Hudson, with Catskill Mountains in Distance," 1840.

Taylor, Eliza Ann (n. d.), Shaker artist, active ca. 1845.

Throop, John Peter Van Ness (1794–ca. 1861) or
Throop, Orramel Hinckley (1798–after 1832) or
Throop, Daniel Scrope (1800–after 1830); all three brothers born at Oxford, New York, to a family with Columbia County connections; they worked at various places in the country as engravers, lithographers, and illustrators. One of them did illustrations for the Hudson publication, *Rural Repository,* 1840s. (p. 111 and 124)

†Tetherly, William (n. d.), fresco painter from New Concord, active ca. 1871.

‡Torrey, Hiram Dwight (1820–1900), landscape painter; born at New Lebanon.

Trumbull, John (1756–1843), portrait and historical painter; influential painter did portraits of county residents.

Tyler, Bayard. (1855–n. d.) portrait painter; late nineteenth century work in Kinderhook.

‡Van Husen, John (probably 1712–after 1756), apprenticed to Raphael Goelet, New York City, 1725–36; born at Claverack; no works identified.

Walgust, Charles (n. d.), landscape painter; view of Columbiaville, 1830. (p.100)

Witzorek, Gus (n. d.), copyist at Kinderhook, 1907. (p.100)

Wall, William Guy (1792–1864), landscape painter; watercolors of Hudson Valley vicinity around Hudson, New York, ca. 1819. (p. 77)

†Walker, Sarah J. (n. d.), amateur landscape painter at North Chatham; probably native born; late nineteenth century.

Wilkie, John (n. d.), portrait painter; Moncrieff Livingston portrait, ca. 1840.

‡Williams, Cuyler J. (1832–1908), landscape painter; born and active at Hillsdale.

†Vanderlyn, John (1775–1852), portrait and historical painter; portrait of Chancellor Robert R. Livingston. (p. 61)

Vanderlyn, Pieter (1687–1778), portrait painter; county portraits of 1730s attributed to him. (p. 36)

The Balance and Columbian Repository. Hudson, New York: Ezra Sampson, George Chittenden, and Harry Croswell, 1802–1808.

The Bee. Hudson, New York: Charles Holt, 1808–19.

Beebe, Lynn, and Davies, Jane B. National Register of Historic Places Inventory — Nomination Form: Bronson (Dr. Oliver) House and Stables. Unpublished descriptive article. Albany, 1973.

Beebe, Lynn. "Teviotdale of Manor Livingston: An Architectural History." Master's thesis, University of Virginia, 1971.

Black, Mary, and Holdridge, Barbara C. and Lawrence B. *Ammi Phillips: Portrait Painter 1788–1865.* New York: Clarkson N. Potter, Inc., 1969.

Black, Mary. *Erastus Salisbury Field's Portrait of his Cousin Lauriette Ashley.* Museum Monographs I. Saint Louis, Missouri: City Art Museum of St. Louis, 1968.

Bonomi, Patricia U. *A Factious People: Politics and Society in Colonial New York.* New York: Columbia University Press, 1971.

Boughton, Mrs. Frederick C., ed. *Historical Booklet: Commemorating Settlement of Canaan Area 1759.* Canaan, New York: Canaan Bi-Centennial Celebration, Inc., 1959.

Bowne, William L. *Ye Cohorn Caravan.* Schuylerville, New York: NaPaul Publishers, Inc., 1975.

Bradbury, Mrs. Anna R. *History of the City of Hudson, New York.* Hudson, New York: Record Printing and Publishing Co., 1908.

Brainard, Homer W. *One of the Gilbert Family of New England: Ancestry of Sarah Rebecca (Gilbert) Bloss, Eighth in Descent from Jonathan Gilbert of Hartford, Connecticut.* Washington, D.C.: Judd & Detweiler, Printers, 1902.

Christman, Henry. *Tin Horns and Calico. 1945.* Reprint. Cornwallville, New York: Hope Farm Press, 1975.

Cikovsky, Nicolai, Jr. *Sanford Robinson Gifford 1823 – 1880.* Catalog. Austin: University of Texas Art Museum, 1970.

Clarkson, Thomas Streatfield. *A Biographical History of Clermont or Livingston Manor.* Clermont, New York: 1869.

Claverack College and Hudson River Institute, Claverack, New York. Descriptive booklet. Claverack, New York: Claverack College and Hudson River Institute, ca. 1895.

Collier, Edward A. *A History of Old Kinderhook.* New York: G. P. Putnam's Sons, 1914.

Collin, John F. *A History of Hillsdale, Columbia County, New York: A Memorabilia of Persons and Things of Interest Passed and Passing.* Philmont, New York: E. J. Beardsley, 1883.

Colvill, Alwyn T. *Old Chatham and Neighbouring Dwellings South of the Berkshires.* The White Pine Series of Architectural Monographs, vol. 5 no. 5 1919.

Corwin, Rev. Edward Tanjore. *A General Ecclesiastical History of Columbia County, New York.* Address delivered at the 60th anniversary of the Reformed Church of Greenport, 1896. Hudson, New York: Hendrick Hudson Chapter, DAR, 1900.

———. *A Manual of the Reformed Church in America. 1628–1878.* 3rd ed., rev. New York: Board of Publication of the Reformed Church in America, 1879.

Crockett, Davy. *The Life of Martin Van Buren.* Philadelphia: Robert Wright, 1835.

Dangerfield, George. *Chancellor Robert R. Livingston of New York 1746–1813.* New York: Harcourt Brace & Company, 1960.

Davies, Jane B. *Papers.* Unpublished memorandum on the Plumb-Bronson house. New York, 1973.

Douglas, Charles Henry James, ed. *A Collection of Family Records with Biographical Sketches and Other Memoranda of Various Families and Individuals Bearing the Name Douglas or Allied to Families of that Name.* Providence: E. L. Freeman, 1879.

Dunlap, William. *History of the Rise and Progress of The Arts of Design in the United States.* 2 vols. 1834. Reprint (3 vols.). New York: Dover Publications, 1969.

Eberlein, Harold D. and Hubbard, Cortlandt Van Dyck. *Historic Houses of the Hudson Valley.* New York: The Architectural Book Publishing Company, 1942.

Ellis, Franklin. *History of Columbia County, New York.* 1878. Reprint. Old Chatham, New York: Sachem Press, 1974.

Fennelly, Catherine. *Textiles in New England, 1750–1840.* Old Sturbridge Village Booklet Series, no. 13. Sturbridge, Massachusetts: Old Sturbridge Village, 1961.

Gayle, Margot, and Gillon, Jr. Edmund V. *Cast-Iron Architecture in New York City. A Photographic Survey.* New York: Dover Publications, 1974.

Gebhard, Elizabeth Louisa. *The Parsonage Between Two Manors: Annals of Clover Reach.* Hudson, New York: Bryan Printing Company, 1925.

Getty, Innes. *The Van Alen Family in America.* New York Genealogical and Biographical Record 81 and 82 New York: 1950 and 1951.

Gray, Maria Sabina (Bogardus). *A Genealogical History of the Ancestors and Descendants of General Robert Bogardus.* Boston: privately printed, 1927.

Griswold, Glenn E., ed. *The Griswold Family: England–America.* Vol. 2. The Griswold Family Association of America Rutland, Vermont: The Tuttle Publishing Company, 1943.

Griswold, Sheldon Munson, and Scovill, William H. *Centennial of Christ Church, Hudson, New York, 1802–1902.* Hudson, New York: Christ Church, 1902.

Groce, George C. and Wallace, David H. *The New York Historical Society's Dictionary of Artists in America, 1564–1860.* New Haven: Yale University Press, 1957.

[Hastings, Hugh]. *Report of the State Historian,* Vol. 2 and 3. 2nd and 3rd Annual Reports transmitted to the legislature. Colonial Series, Vols. 1 and 2. Albany and New York: Wynkoop Hollenbeck Crawford Co., 1896 and 1897.

Howat, John K. *The Hudson River and Its Painters:* New York: Viking Press, 1972.

Hudson Female Academy. *Fourth Annual Catalogue of the Hudson Female Academy.* Hudson, New York: Hudson Female Academy, 1855.

Hudson Gazette, ed. *Columbia County at the End of the Century.* 2 vols. Hudson, New York: Hudson Gazette, 1900.

Hunt, Thomas. *A Historical Sketch of the Town of Clermont.* Hudson, New York: Privately printed, 1928.

Huntington, David C. Introduction to *Frederic Edwin Church.* Catalog of an exhibition, Smithsonian publication 4657. Washington, D. C.: National Collection of Fine Arts, Smithsonian Institution, 1966.

Jacobus, Donald Lines, and Waterman, Edgar Francis. *The Waterman Family. Volume III. Descendants of Richard Waterman of Providence, Rhode Island.* Hartford: E. F. Waterman, 1954.

Johnson, Sir William. *The Papers of Sir William Johnson.* Edited by James Sullivan and Alexander Flick, 14 vols. Albany: The University of the State of New York, 1921–65.

Jones, Agnes Halsey. *Rediscovered Artists of Upstate New York 1700–1875.* Catalog of an exhibition. Utica: Munson-Proctor-Williams Institute, 1958.

Kenney, Alice P. *The Gansevoorts of Albany: Dutch Patricians in the Upper Hudson Valley.* Syracuse, New York: Syracuse University Press, 1969.

Kimball, Fiske. *Domestic Architecture of the America Colonies and the Early Republic. 1922.* Reprint. New York: Dover Publications, 1966.

Knittle, Walter Allen. *Early Eighteenth Century Palatine Emigration. 1937.* Reprint. Baltimore: Genealogical Publishing Co., 1965.

Lassiter, William L. *Shaker Architecture*. New York: Vantage Press, 1966.

Lipman, Jean. "An Early Masonic Meeting Place." *Antiques,* May 1949: 355–357.

Livingston, Edwin Brockholst. *The Livingstons of Livingston Manor*. New York: Privately printed, 1910.

McNamee, Daniel V., Jr. *If You Remember*. Monographs on Columbia County. Hudson, New York: Evening Register Press, 1936.

Mann, Maybelle. *Francis William Edmonds*. Introduction and catalog. Washington, D. C.: International Exhibitions Foundations, 1975.

Miller, Peyton F. *A Group of Great Lawyers of Columbia County*. New York: Privately printed, 1904.

Miller, Stephen B. *Historical Sketches of Hudson*. Hudson, New York: Bryan & Webb Printers, 1862.

Minick, Rachel. "Henry Ary, and Unknown Painter of the Hudson River School." *Bulletin: The Brooklyn Museum,* vol. 2, no. 4: 14–24.

Moore, Horace L. *Andrew Moore of Poquonock and Windsor, Connecticut, and His Descendants*. Lawrence, Kansas: Journal Publishing Company, 1903.

Olmstead, Elizabeth W., ed. *Selections from the Correspondence and Diaries of John Olmstead 1826–1838*. Buffalo: Privately published, 1968.

Pearson, Jonathan and Van Laer, Arnold J. F., trans. and ed. *Early Records of the City and County of Albany and Colony of Rensselaerwyck*. 4 vols. Albany: The University of the State of New York, 1865 and 1916–19.

Pettit, Florence H. *America's Printed and Painted Fabrics*. New York: Hasting House, 1970.

Polakoff, Keith Ian. *The Politics of Inertia. The Election of 1876 and the End of Reconstruction*. Baton Rouge: Louisiana State University Press, 1973.

Polk, James, Masters, Hillary; Langdon, Olive; Lusardi, Richard; and Hunt, Margaret. *A History of the Roeliff Jansen Area*. Columbia County, New York: The Roeliff Jansen Historical Society, 1975.

Quimby, Ian M. G., ed. *American Painting to 1776: A Reappraisal*. Winterthur Conference Report. Charlottesville, Virginia: University of Virginia Press, 1971.

Raymond, William. *Biographical Sketches of the Distinguished Men of Columbia County, including and Account of the Most Important Offices They Have Filled, in the State and General Governments, and in the Army and Navy*. Albany: Weed, Parsons, & Co., 1851.

Reiff, Daniel D. *Architecture in Fredonia*. Catalog of an exhibit. Fredonia: The Michael C. Rockefeller Arts Center Gallery, State University College and The Lakeshore Association for the Arts, 1972.

Reynolds, Helen Wilkinson. *Dutch Houses in the Hudson Valley Before 1776*. 1929. Reprint. New York: Dover Publications, 1965.

Rockefeller, Henry Oscar, ed. *Rockefeller Genealogy*. Vol. 4. New York: Rockefeller Family Association, ca. 1940.

Runk, Emma Ten Broeck. *The Ten Broeck Genealogy: Being the Records and Annals of Dirck Wesselse Ten Broeck of Albany and His Descendants*. New York: Privately printed, 1897.

Ru̇ral Repository. Hudson, New York: William B. Stoddard, 1824–51.

Saunders, Randall. *Remember Claverack College*. Hudson, New York: Hudson Evening Register, 1944.

Silliman, B[enjamin]. *Remarks Made on a Short Tour between Hartford and Quebec in the Autumn of 1819*. 2nd ed. rev. New Haven: S. Converse, 1824.

Sloane Eric. *American Barns and Covered Bridges*. New York: W. Funk, 1954.

Smith, William. *Historical Memoirs of William Smith from 12 July 1776 to 25 July 1778*. Edited by William H. W. Sabine, Hollis, Long Island, New York: Colburn & Tegg, 1958.

Spafford, Horatio Gates, LL.D. *A Gazetteer of the State of New York*. Albany: B. D. Packard, 1824.

Stokes, Olivia E. Phelps. *Letters and Memories of Susan and Ann Bartlett Warner*. New York and London: G. P. Putnam's Sons, 1925.

Sullivan, James, ed. *Minutes of the Albany Committee of Correspondence, 1775–1778*. 2 vols. Albany: The University of the State of New York, 1923.

Terry, Robert M., ed. *The "Hudsonian." Old Times and New. A Home Record of Historical Sketches pertaining to the City of Hudson, and its Immediate Vicinity*. Hudson, New York: Published by the author, 1895.

Torrey, Jesse, Jun. *The Intellectual Torch. Developing a Plan for the Universal Dissemination of Knowledge and Virtue by Means of Free Public Libraries*. The Librarian's Series. No. 3. Edited by John Cotton Dana and Henry W. Kent, Woodstock, Vermont: Elm Tree Press, 1912.

———. *Portraiture of Slavery*. Philadelphia: Published by the author, 1817.

Travers, George W. *A Century of Brewing. Hudson Ales and the Evans Brewery, a History for One Hundred Years*. New York: The Moss Engraving Company, 1886.

Upjohn, Everard M. *Richard Upjohn: Architect and Churchman*. New York: Columbia University Press, 1939.

Van Alstine, Lester. *Van Alstyne-Van Alstine Family History*. Vol. 1. Salem, Wisconsin: Published by the author, 1974.

Van Laer, Arnold J. F. See Pearson, Jonathan and Van Laer, Arnold J. F. *Early Records of the City and county of Albany and Colony of Rensselaerwyck*.

———.trans. and ed. *Correspondence of Jeremias Van Rensselaer, 1652–1674*. The University of the State of New York, 1932.

———.trans. and ed. *Correspondence of Maria Van Rensselaer 1669–1689*. Albany: The University of the State of New York, 1935.

Van Rensselaer, Florence. *The Livingston Family in America and Its Scottish Origins*. Arr. by William Laimbeer. New York: Privately printed, 1949.

———. and FitzRandolph, Ethel L. *The Van Rensselaers in Holland and In America*. New York: Privately printed, 1956.

Van Schaack, Henry C., "An Old Kinderhook Mansion." *The American Magazine of History* 2: 513–28.

———. *The Life of Peter Van Schaack, LL.D., Embracing Selections from His Correspondence and Other Writings, during the American Revolution, and His Exile in England*. New York: D. Appleton & Co. 1842.

———. *Memoirs of the Life of Henry Van Schaack*. Chicago: A. C. McClurg & Company, 1892.

Van Vleck, Jane. *The Ancestry and Descendants of Teilman Van Vleck of Nieuw Amsterdam*. New York: Privately printed, 1955.

Waterman, Edgar Francis, and Jacobus, Donald Lines. *The Waterman Family. Volumes I and II. Descendants of Robert Waterman of Marshfield, Massachusetts*. New Haven: E. F. Waterman, 1939 and 1943.

Webb, F. H. *Claverack Old and New*. Claverack, 1892.

Whittelsey, Charles B. *The Ancestry and Descendants of John Pratt of Hartford, Connecticut, 1538–1900*. Hartford: The Case, Lockwood & Brainard Co., 1900.

Woodbridge, Timothy. *Autobiography of a Blind Minister*. Boston: John P. Jewett and Company, 1856.

Worth, Gorham A. [Ignatius Jones]. "Recollections of Hudson." In *Random Recollections of Albany from 1800 to 1808: With Some Additional Matter*. 2nd ed. Albany: Charles Van Benthuysen, 1850.

Zabriskie, Rev. Francis Nicoll. *History of the Reformed P. D. Church of Claverack: A Centennial Address*. Hudson: S. B. Miller, 1867.

Manuscripts

Albany, New York. Albany County Deeds, vols. 4–9. Clerk's Office, Albany County Courthouse.

———.Land Papers; Lansing Collection; Powers Family Papers; Sylvester Papers; Warshaw Collection; and miscellaneous manuscripts indexed under surnames and place names. New York State Library.

———. Hendryk Van Rensselaer's Account Book. Albany Institute of History and Art, McKinney Library.

Hudson, New York. Columbia County Deeds, misc. volumes beginning with "A." Clerk's Office, Columbia County Courthouse.

Champlain, New York. McLellan Collection of Pliny Moore Papers.

Kinderhook, New York. Hinds Collection; Van Buren Collection; and miscellaneous manuscripts catalogues by surname and place names. Columbia County Historical Society Library.